W0246881

EBURY PRESS
# WHITE AS MILK AND RICE

Nidhi Dugar Kundalia is a journalist. Her stories have appeared in various national newspapers and magazines. She mostly writes on socio-cultural issues, documenting human lives and their journeys through various settings. Her first book, *The Lost Generation: Chronicling India's Dying Professions*, was released in 2016 to a warm reception. She is a graduate of the School of Arts, City University, London, and lives in Kolkata with her husband and children.

ALSO BY THE SAME AUTHOR

*The Lost Generation*

## ADVANCE PRAISE FOR THE BOOK

'The hamlets of India are the bedrock of fantastic untold stories that make us wonder. In this book, Nidhi goes to remote villages with the courage of an adventurous journalist and tells us life stories we have not heard. The beautiful and poetic language makes the book heart-warming; the stories linger long after reading them. I suggest this book as one of the must-haves on your reading shelf, and in our libraries'—**Benyamin**, author of *Goat Days*

'Nidhi Dugar Kundalia does justice to the arduous task of chronicling the lives of six tribal communities from India's heartland as she writes about their intimate moments and interactions with the outside world, their pains and celebrations, beliefs and wisdom. She tempers her surprise and curiosity with empathy and fine writing, producing a book that does not intrude like a voyeur but places the reader in the midst of these people like a benign eyewitness'—**Hansda Sowvendra Shekhar**, author of *The Adivasi Will Not Dance*

'I made a documentary film on the tribal communities of Bastar titled *Close to Nature* exactly fifty-two years ago. At the time, the cultural practices and lifestyles of the Maria and the Muria communities of both the plateaus and the plains had barely changed from the time their history began to be recorded. This was largely due to their semi-isolated existence in difficult-to-reach forested areas, almost untouched but altogether surrounded by our ever-expanding agrarian/industrializing world. It took no more than a couple of decades for their entire way of life to be radically altered, if not altogether obliterated, leaving behind detritus in the form of desperately poor and helpless communities that have been forever exploited and pushed to the bottom of the civilizational pyramid. Change overtook these communities with drastic suddenness, their fragile cultures unable to withstand the pressure of our rapidly urbanizing civilization. *White as Milk and Rice* has engrossing tales that are told with genuine feeling and beautiful details of constantly evolving human emotions. There are books that change the way you look at people, and this is one of them'—**Shyam Benegal**, film-maker and screenwriter

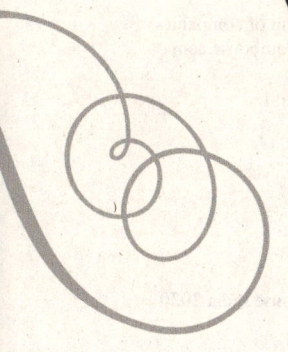

# WHITE
## AS
# MILK
## AND
# RICE

*Stories of India's Isolated Tribes*

# nidhi dugar kundalia

EBURY
PRESS

An imprint of Penguin Random House

EBURY PRESS

USA | Canada | UK | Ireland | Australia
New Zealand | India | South Africa | China | Singapore

Ebury Press is part of the Penguin Random House group of companies
whose addresses can be found at global.penguinrandomhouse.com

Published by Penguin Random House India Pvt. Ltd
4th Floor, Capital Tower 1, MG Road,
Gurugram 122 002, Haryana, India

Penguin
Random House
India

First published in Ebury Press by Penguin Random House India 2020

Copyright © Nidhi Dugar Kundalia 2020

All rights reserved

10 9 8 7 6 5 4 3 2

The views and opinions expressed in this book are the author's own and the facts
are as reported by her which have been verified to the extent possible, and the
publishers are not in any way liable for the same.

ISBN 9780143429470

Typeset in Adobe Garamond Pro by Manipal Technologies Limited, Manipal

Printed at Manipal Technologies Limited, India

This book is sold subject to the condition that it shall not, by way of trade
or otherwise, be lent, resold, hired out, or otherwise circulated without the
publisher's prior consent in any form of binding or cover other than that in
which it is published and without a similar condition including this condition
being imposed on the subsequent purchaser.

www.penguin.co.in

MIX
Paper | Supporting
responsible forestry
FSC® C043100

This is a legitimate digitally printed version of the book and therefore might not
have certain extra finishing on the cover.

*To my husband,*
*for fostering my grit*

# CONTENTS

# CONTENTS

# INTRODUCTION

Early on in my journalistic career, I met a young woman who called herself Birsu. She was quietly holding a placard at a rally outside the collector's office in Narayanpur, Chhattisgarh, the only woman in a group of men protesting mining activity close to their village. I discreetly jotted down her address, avoiding the prying eyes of the constable accompanying me—the police accompanying journalists is the norm in Bastar. The next day, when I arrived in the village where she lived and went looking for her, I found, to my dismay, that there was no one by that name. After hours of searching, I gave up and started the journey back in my taxi. I saw her then, piling firewood in the thickets outside the village. She looked surprised and remarked, 'I didn't think you would come. No one ever comes back to us.' She had given me a false name. But I continued calling her Birsu in my story on the Marias.

Over the course of that one week that I travelled through the state, I spent my nights in a government guesthouse

in Narayanpur, and most of my days in her village. Birsu
let me into her life only after we negotiated a great deal
of mutual mistrust, and we carefully sieved through her
story. She was not a part of the Naxalite movement, but
often made meals for the cadre when they came visiting
at night; over the years, she had developed for them not
only fear but also respect, for unlike her villagers, they were
brave and hard-working, fighting for what they thought
was theirs.

Days later, when I returned home, I trawled through
books and libraries for more on Birsu's tribe.

I was quickly disenchanted by the available material:
it was either a record of their cultural history before
Independence with a focus on overly decorated dance and
song, or miserable pictures of their dismal conditions.
For me, the intrigue lay in the life they had been leading
post-Independence. How has the changing environment
and economy of India affected them? How has their
movement outwards from the isolated depths of the forests
and remote mountains, and the partial integration with the
rest of society, changed them? How do these changes affect
individuals? Do they bring these individuals into conflict
with the larger goals of their tribal societies and villages?
What I was hoping for was, perhaps, more humane sketches
of Birsu's people.

I was looking for a book that would begin to answer
some of my questions, because I felt I could not write about
them myself—not being a tribal, not having a lifetime of
knowledge on the subject and not knowing most of their

languages. There were statistics and government data on their health, education etc.; it contradicted their narratives and often completely overlooked tribals living in isolated corners. I felt there was a shortage of writing on the subject that dealt with them not as socio-political subjects or cultural objects, but delved deeper into the lives they have lived in the past few decades—a history of their emotional evolution post-Independence, their changing relationship with outsiders, their relationships with the environment and with their own people: husbands, wives, lovers, parents and children. In short, their life stories.

The Marias and other tribals that I had come to know across the country were not bizarre and definitely not pitiable. They had adapted, and are rapidly adapting, to the fast-changing conditions around them, mostly at the cost of their traditional lives and livelihoods.

I decided to try writing a chronicle of this sort, conducting dozens of interviews at length with various tribal communities. The translators, the subjects of the interviews and others who helped establish the contexts of the six tribal stories I wrote for this book articulated the effects of their changing lives and patterns of living. These six tribals were unassuming people who were barely used to any attention, forget that of the media.

In no way do I claim that these individuals represent the whole tribe. I thought it would be useful to follow one or two individuals of each of these tribes over the course of a few weeks to create an account of their lives. We talked through an interpreter, but only after overcoming our differences of class and gender. Then there was the usual research, which involved scholarly articles, papers, maps and pictures. I was acutely aware of my non-tribal background when I spoke to them, but I tried to compensate by being a good listener. More importantly, it took patience as they assessed their own feelings and formulated sentences. Above all, I took notes on their silences.

Just as stories of these individuals are not representative of their entire tribes, they are not even a sum total of their individual lives. In every village, every household and even with every individual, details differ, and that matters. The Khasi sisters I write about refused to convert to Christianity like most of their generation; the Kanjar gangster surrendered to the police but still brews illegal liquor for sale while many of his ilk in other villages practise, in Kanjari parlance, 'truck cutting', or looting trucks; the Kurumba boy took to arms more easily than to government schooling, unlike a lot of his peers. And yet, largely, their stories echo similar thoughts.

Through their life stories I have woven in texture, not forgetting the environment, which varied so vastly from story to story and lent itself to the characters and personalities of my protagonists. Where I think information has interfered with the storytelling, I have added it in footnotes and endnotes.

The process of the interview itself was not without its pitfalls. A lot was lost in translation, and the translators often hid details because they were ashamed or didn't think they mattered to an outsider. I frequently made a fool of myself, asking what seemed to them rather obvious, especially the everyday things about their culture. There were incidents and emotions that they aggressively chose to forget and deliberately reframed, to move on with their lives or fearing authorities or simply to gain control, as they attempted to outline their lives once again on their own terms.

Identity issues among these tribals are deep-rooted due to the years of injustice meted out to them. Take the instance of the Alu Kurumbas: Back in 1901, when Thurston first conducted a study on the Kurumba tribe in the Nilgiris, the prefix 'Alu' was absent; it seems to have been a recent development, a phenomenon just a few decades old. 'Alu' in Kannada means milk, implying good and harmless like milk. Before this, the tribe was feared due to their sorcery and witchcraft practices, and it deprived them of employment, education and integration and interaction with the other tribes in the region. It is quite possible that in order to remove or impair the negative opinion the local people entertained of them, certain sections of the Kurumbas themselves might have added the new prefix of Alu for improved status and wider acceptability. Another tribe documented in this book, the Halakkis, subjected to years of antipathy from mainstream society, credits its name to the rice they grow, which is white as milk. The title *White as Milk and Rice*, hence, is not irrelevant to the theme of the book.

Each time a new set of invaders charged into the Indian subcontinent, the Indian tribals were pushed further back into the shadows, where they learnt to survive on what was available. Subsequently, they came to be called 'savages'. In the recent past, thanks to modern encroachments and development, they have been forced back into 'civilized' society, which they neither understood nor were prepared for.

Post Independence, Jawaharlal Nehru formulated the Panchsheel principles, meant to guide government actions in dealing with tribal people. More recently, PESA (the Panchayats [Extension to the Scheduled Areas) Act], 1996, and the Forests Rights Act, 2006, have made a difference. But tribals in the interiors are largely unaware of their rights. On paper, these acts are intended to protect 'tribals' against mainstream society, strengthening 'tribal' cultural institutions, while at the same time furthering their integration with mainstream society. However, well-intended these measures are, their goals seem to be contradictory, resulting in policies that in one way or another have only complicated their circumstances.

Organizations representing these tribal communities in central, south and north-east India unite them as 'first people' and claim that they are 'indigenous' to India. The presumption is then that present-day Adivasis or 'tribes' are distinct cultural communities, historically marginalized, or are descendants of the 'original' inhabitants of a given territory. Political movements and media that build on these claims tend to further objectify the cultural characteristics of these communities: ancestral rituals become performances; photographs of their clothes and jewellery are pictured as symbols of 'tribality'. Mostly, such images are far removed from their earlier setting; contemporary displays tend to be sentimentalized imaginations that have gained prominence due to specific historical and political circumstances. Again, that does not mean that the people who belong to the communities do not share certain distinguishing pasts, habits and cultural practices.

But as a fallout, we are now confined in a zero-sum game: If the government is wrong, the rebels must be right or the other way around. In this protracted conflict, the tribals seem to be the biggest victim.

The fact is tribals have their own design of development. For instance, the Konyak villages in Nagaland have an incredible community-led system in which the village council periodically assigns groups of young men and women to work in the villagers' fields, irrespective of who owns them, and to work together for all social occasions such as weddings, funerals and festivals. In the Gondi language of the Marias, there is no future tense because their lives function around the availability of the natural resources around them: land, forests and water. Here is where the conflict lies: People outside their world want to get those resources and impose new development models on them.

Over the last few decades, rapid urbanization has affected the character of their lives; the loss of their innocence and the damage to their environment are, perhaps, irreversible. As the country grapples with new laws, climate changes and policies, these marginalized lives serve as a dire warning.

*White as Milk and Rice* is, then, my humble attempt to not bring this margin to the centre, but to make the margin a place of reality.

# 1

# THE HALAKKIS OF ANKOLA

*The singing women of the Halakki tribe*

Ankola, Karnataka

Last night, Sukri could not sleep. Lying on her mattress, she gazed at the palm roof, listening to the rooster crow; it probably mistook the moon for the sun when it reappeared after a long time. She had hoped to hear her mother—her everyday music—but there was no blowing on the fire or tinkling anklets, no sharpening of the sickle on the stone. A hairy tarantula inched up the wall before her. Sukri watched it aim for a beetle, and just when it was about to grab its prey, she rapped her knuckles on the cow dung–coated walls, sending the spider scampering up to the palm roof and beyond.

The lighthouse keeper who lived by the sea close to their village appeared in her thoughts again. He had done that whenever Sukri had nothing else to do, ever since he had caught her behind the lighthouse, playing in a broken boat with a stranded frog, and told her, 'Wasting your time like this? One day, you'll be swept away by the waters like this boat and never be found.' In the nights, when the moon rises into the high skies, the waves fill up the cold cavity of the boat, small black fish knocking against its walls. The beach is quiet and empty on such nights except for the solitary lighthouse keeper, updating his logs in the lighthouse as it spins the light. When it stops just before dawn, the darkness swallows the boat whole.

This morning, minutes after the first light pours on to the beach, Sukri walks out with a mud pot and a knife. Her mother, with a few other women from their village, must have already reached the forests to gather wood. At the sea, the water still has the beach short. The waves open out as they rise, white rolls unwinding, smashing against rock, sand, the broken boat and the lighthouse far up on the beach.

Soon, women in short saris that fall till just below their knees pick the stockfish in their palms, let the water run through their fingers and deposit the slippery fish in the pots. The sun shines on their bare, dark backs. The beach is crowded today. Last night was a new moon, so the tide was at its highest and plenty of crabs came ashore. Most people pick up the crabs, while some chip away the mussels that cling to coastal rocks. Other girls from Sukri's village join in: Gowri, who sits beside Sukri, is to be married soon. She will come of age[1] any time now and her parents are already exchanging gifts with the groom's family. Parvathi, dislodging the tiny molluscs from their shells, complains, 'I want to get married tomorrow. All my friends from the village are married.' Sukri's mother had told her that their father had chosen a boy for her, but all Sukri really wanted to do was go to school—use paper, pen and inkpot to write long verses. She wasn't yet sure what she would write, but the pages would be filled with blue ink. 'Words are unnecessary,' her mother insisted. 'We work in the fields and forests; what use are our words to us?' Moreover, her father needed the *tara* or the bride price, her mother added, pretending that this was an afterthought.

'They took away Bighu's land yesterday,' one grandmother tells another, pulling out a splinter of wood that stabs her as she hunts for crabs among the rocks. 'They cut his thumb and stamped the document. He owed them some money.'

'Hmm.' Another nods. 'Even Chenchu's land was taken away last month. He has only a boat and nine fingers left to feed his family.'

'Fingers or no fingers, it is us women who have to feed our children. With little pieces of this *chiplikali*,' a young woman adds, examining the tiny molluscs floating in her pot. 'The men can go sulk at the wine shops on the highway.' She mumbles something wearily, her mouth and breasts drooping from suckling her youngest two. Whether or not her husband has asked her to, she has obligingly taken on the duty of both father and mother: getting firewood from the forest; tilling others' lands; feeding her four children and paying for his alcohol. He is the man, so he is the master. 'It is the way it should be.' The young woman shrugged.

Sukri thinks of her father, who has already sold half of his land to the Nadavaru man. Last night, when he did not come back home, her mother asked her to go looking for him at the toddy shop. Sukri had sat beside the boat instead; it wasn't for scorekeeping or revenge, it had taken on a redemptive implication for her. She wouldn't have to refuse paying for his liquor then. Her submissiveness would negate her father's fierce need to combat the threat of being disciplined by a daughter.

For a while, no one says anything at the beach. Only their bangles jingle against each other. Women here in Shirkuli, a village in Ankola district, love glass bangles; they are allowed to wear them on the left hand. The bangles could, after all, break into the food that they cook and serve to their husbands with their right. In the silence, Sukri hears the waves rushing to the shore at the speed of her thoughts. She watches the sea release tiny armies of crabs, which quickly rush back to the sea, where the threat of being washed away is equal to the threat of being killed, where the most fragile of living flesh must withstand the waves that are strong enough to change the shape of an abyss and move continents. But again, Sukri and the mussels, oysters and barnacles all owe their lives, and their food, to these currents.

As she works, she slowly starts humming, mostly out of habit. The others begin to hum too. They, the Halakki tribals, sing[2] so often that they don't realize they are doing it. They sing when they are content, when they are anxious, when they are sad; many songs in the same tune, with no formal knowledge of music.

'*Channa edige mette chenche tumbe . . .*'[3]

The song is about a group of women on a boat with the sun looming over it, and the boatman rowing it into the sea. Sukri secretly hopes to get on one of these fishermen's boats and travel to faraway lands. Everyone sings along as they work about these women of the Konkan coast, who always carry *chenche*—a bag that holds their favourite pastime of betel leaves and areca nuts, chewed between those hours of work. The bag is also used to hide money or precious objects like a small piece of gold. The women continue singing about the valuable chenche bag, which suddenly slips into the water. The disheartened women of the song beg the boatman to dive in and find it. This bag is so precious that, in return, a woman promises him a *kalungra*, her silver toe ring, her sign of marriage.

\* \* \*

Not much has changed over the years. The cool cow dung flooring still heals Sukri's toes after a long day at work and the *valle* always has hot water to bathe in. Her husband's house in Badageri, in the Ankola district, has tiles alongside the palm rafters these days. The laterite stone walls, made from the sand at the beach, have shells here and there; if you listen closely, they echo the sea and its waves. But mostly, Sukri's dark hut resonates with the sounds of her husband, gracelessly ensconced in this square hut. Living with him for over a decade has taught her all his sounds: the moaning, churning, leaking of a body struggling to outlive its time.

He is about to die. She is used to death by now; her two children died soon after they were born. When her second child succumbed to sickness and her husband fell ill, she was sure he'd be all right soon. Since she had just lost her two offspring, she could not possibly lose her husband this soon; the custodians of fate were not that cruel. She massages the pain from her husband's chest in the dark till he begins to take slow, deep breaths, and then tiptoes across the floor to get into her mattress with her dirty feet. Everyone else lives near the market. Theirs is among the few *koppas*[4] close to the forest. Usually, her only companions are the animals: the foxes, the mongoose and the cats prowling the edge of the forest. She thinks of the fox chasing a rabbit; the mongoose and cats slinking up the tree. She waits to hear their calls. But the animals are not there; they have already fled deep into the forest.

Sukri was married when she was sixteen to her forty-five-year-old bridegroom, Bommagowda, whom she had never seen before that. While she wore silver bangles, he had worn nothing but a loincloth when he first came with his parents and paid the bride price. On the wedding day, her uncles gave betel leaf and areca nut to the groom's relatives[5] and put up a pergola[6] with leaves, coconut plumes and dry paper flowers. The women had made *halli*[7] on the walls, connecting small dots with patterns and other icons like parrots, marking the places where the groom and bride would sit. The corner was then adorned with flowers from bushes around their homes: jasmine, margosa, hibiscus and chrysanthemum.

She returned to her parents' home for a day after the wedding. Her mother handed her a gold ring in a chenche. 'For troubled times,' she said prophetically, blinking back tears. More women from the neighbourhood surrounded them, singing ritual farewell songs that soon turned into mischievous jingles, mocking an eager husband waiting for his wife on the first night, and then poking fun at her in-laws with some not-so-polite commentary on a mother-in-law.

'*Neerige chepuna chepana . . .*'

'We went to the in-laws' place,' they sang, 'and they did not offer us any jaggery.' Halakkis usually drink water with a small piece of jaggery to quench their thirst; this drink is offered to guests too. Special occasions call for a concoction of powdered ragi, lentils and sesame served with jaggery. Some of them, though, have started offering tea, calling it the 'watery-milk drink'. The song continues: 'The in-laws did not offer any jaggery with water. How niggardly was that! We have watering wells in our village too, so why do we care about the plain water that they served us?'

The Halakkis's *janapada*, or folk songs, were never accompanied by instruments. They were always sung by women in groups of three or four, Sukri sensed early on. Men went to the fields or worked for Nadavas[8] or the Havyakas, working as labourers in their fields and homes. In their free time, they either drank the local brew *nausagara*[9] or played, the drum. Women, on the other hand, hardly had any free hours, what with gathering the forest produce in the morning, working in the fields in the afternoon, and in the evening, selling the produce in the markets. At the end of the day, they finished their cooking and cleaning and tended to the cattle and their children.

The janapadas also had their own version of the
epics: Mahabharat was known as *Pandavakami* and the
Ramayana, they called *Seethekami*. According to the songs
that Sukri sings, it was not Ram but Lakshman who won
Seetha. Lakshman did not break any magical bow to win
Seetha; he killed a crow that interrupted her father King
Janak's meditation. The songs of tribal Ramayana contain
wonderful descriptions, like that of a spider forming a
cobweb in the throat of Lakshman, who resolves not to
touch food or water for the sake of his elder brother. During
the days of the Suggi festival, Sukri sometimes sings these
songs all night. She is aware that, unlike in other versions,
for the Halakkis, Seetha is the glorious protagonist instead
of Ram, turning the epic into her story of love and struggle.
The songs speak of Seetha's fondness for trees, animals and
forests in an oracular way, describing a series of difficult,
painful settings in her life. Often, as Sukri sings these songs,
and the powerful imagery wells up her eyes, she forgets that
these songs are about Seetha's life, not hers.

\* \* \*

Early the next day, Sukri heats the water to mix with ragi
and buttermilk for *ambli*, placing a glass of it before her
sleeping husband. She drapes a sari around her bosom like
a sarong, keeping the back bare. The Nadavaru women,
wives of landowners and moneylenders, who lived in
Ankola town, wore blouses beneath their saris like the
women of Bengaluru. Maybe because they had underarm
hair, Sukri assumed. No woman in Badageri had hair

there growing like stubby, dry grass. Some newly married Halakki would sometimes ape them, hoping to elevate her status to those of the higher-caste Nadavarus. But she liked her back bare,[10] which let her sweat cool to the breeze beneath the burning Konkan sun.

By dawn, Sukri joins three other women on their way to the forest, their hips swinging below the dark, bare backs given up to the rising sun. All four wear silver *halkaddis*[11] and *gutki mani*: layers of colourful beads around their neck, all the way down to the shoulder. Made of polished sand grains and strung on threads of pineapple leaves, their favourite beads are coloured yellow, black and Prussian blue. They put them on for each other, layering them, letting the beads intermingle, which, like a turban, support their necks when they carry firewood on their heads. Their middle-parted hair is oiled; a pendulous bun is adorned with the red *abbalige* or white jasmine flowers plucked fresh every morning. Each of them has a silver nose pin, the *mugati*. Widows cannot wear them, and Sukri wonders, as she puts it on, whom she would give this nose pin to when her husband died.

The women prefer this long walk to the forest to facing the dirty pots and pans of the night before or the hot paddy fields. Sukri relishes the quiet calm, watching the mist that covers the forest slowly dissipate with the rising sun. The path into the Sahyadri forest stretches out on both sides of the road, darkly, politely, occasionally tapering into a chute so tight that tree branches hang over their heads like bridges. Mostly, they choose the left side of the highway, with beaten paths and known obstacles. Today, they take the right side, just to venture on to a different path. But this everyday ritual, of collecting the firewood, wild crop manure and cane, they never miss.

Years ago, they were surprised when government officials with tags around their necks came down to the village and forced them to take a day off for a certain 'skills development programme'. They had never taken a day off from the forests and fields unless it was during the Suggi[12] festival. One of the women, in a crisp saree and fitted blouse, stood up at the gathering, held under a wild fig tree in Ankola, and said, 'I came to teach you how to make kokum butter. Do you know how much that thing sells for now?' Sukri was staring at the plastic folders with the then chief minister's vapid smile plastered on it. They ate the government-sponsored chicken curry for lunch and drank free tea all day and later that evening, they laughed raucously. Kokum butter–making was a process every girl in Ankola and beyond knew from her mother's womb.

Kokum butter might be quick money, but no woman in Ankola district would choose more hours at home to these morning forest visits.

'It rained last night,' Ganga tells her daughter Sita, who has recently started accompanying them to the forest. 'On dry days, we can find mature wood just by its smell.'

'Sita! You've grown like a ragi sprout,' Sukri tells the young girl, engaged to be married soon.[13]

'It's been a long time, uh?' Sukri continues. 'I heard from your mother you cook well. Did you bring me anything to eat?'

'No, akka,' Sita said.

'Sita, you thoughtless girl.' She laughs and the other older women join her in the cackle, officially welcoming Sita to their posse.

'*Chanda da matgai . . .*' Sita begins to sing as they walk into the Sahyadri forest. Sukri closes her eyes momentarily and then joins her as her soul thrums with the familiar notes of the folk song. The verses speak of the abundant Sahyadri forest, tying the firewood obtained from it and taking it back home. Sita has a raw, untrained voice that is soft and mossy. She stretches the vowels towards the end while at least two or three other women provide backing chorus. Occasionally, for a note or two, she and other singers fall into perfect harmony, and when that happens, Sukri feels elated, as if she has discovered a new reason to be happy.

Sukri smiles to herself. When did this song, which her mother composed when they went to the forest, pass on? How did it last so far from the place of her mother's birth?

Sukri remembers the first time she accompanied her mother, Devi, to the paddy fields along with her younger sisters when she was six or eight. Devi used to wear more beads than Sukri, her favourite being a row of yellow amid black. Her mother had a song for every plant or tree on their way. As a little girl, Sukri would drink in the blue sky, the scarecrow and the fields that stretched for miles without making much sense of it. On seeing a snake, the *kerehau*, she would nudge it with a foot. The Halakki elders said that unless a snake shows its venom, little children will turn it over, play with it using the hands, and women will use it for tying firewood.

On one of those afternoons, Sukri had made up her own song about a snake without realizing it: 'Kaage matu Haavu . . .'

'Crazy girl Sukki, what are you gabbling?' rebuked her mother. Sukri almost bit her tongue in shame, but pretended to squint up in concentration, as though looking for ripening mangoes was more important than what her mother was saying.

Basava Gowda had divided the work in the fields, bossing the women around:

'Move your hands faster!'

'Look at you, weeding out my crop. I don't have granaries full of rice that you can waste this . . .'

'You stinking wild animal,' he chided another, who was discreetly packing the weeds in her basket for her cattle. 'Did I employ you to steal me blind? You know how expensive fodder is? How would you know? You earn easy money from me . . .'

Sukri had weeded along with her mother, pulling out junglerice and toothcup as the heat came to the afternoon, convincing and copious. A row of red ants crawled around her feet, disappearing in and out of the red mud. Sukri made up another song:

'Red ants, those that march up your legs and make red marks on your bottom . . .'

This time, Devi had let her sing. Along with the gold bangles Devi made for her, she would take these songs to her in-laws' place, and they would see her through long hours of work. Every day, they would sing these songs along with other labourers in the fields and often, the little Sukri would fall asleep halfway through the weeding, under the cool shade of a mango tree. One day, Sukri and her mother sat in a bus and went to Mysore to see the Dussehra festival. The last crowned king, Jayachamarajendra Wadiyar himself, had led the procession, seated on a golden howdah on the royal elephant's back, followed by long rows of horses, elephants decked in gold, and performances by puppeteers and dancers. On the bus back home, Devi and Sukri sang a song about horses and the golden howdah on which the king sat. Sukri now missed how time had seemed to stand still back then, if only for a few post-dusk breaths; the sun softened enough to look at it directly from the window.

They whispered their songs so that non-Halakkis on the bus couldn't hear them. Devi could be stingy like that, keeping her ancestral songs locked inside her ribcage. She'd rather let them die than have them parodied. They hummed their favourite, the one they sang on Mondays while offering prayers to the tulsi shrub in their yard:

*Eh nath tulasi garo*
*Atalo chomein garodalo*
*Cheralo atalochomein garodanalo*
(Addressing Goddess Tulsi, we have brought flower and doll.

All of it we have brought to you, and *chandanna*
*srigandha*, sandalwood paste.
Tulsamma, each doll we will decorate, to please you we
are doing all this.)

\* \* \*

Sita sings the Tulsamma song as they walk in the forest,
crunching bark and leaves beneath them. Why did they
all know the chorus to these songs? Sukri wonders. They
had inherited these songs orally, rather than in written
form. Often, the meaning of the colloquial, ancient words
escapes them, but they sing it for the sorority—songs that
bind them together through their hardships, but songs
Sukri associates only with happiness, with festivals, forests,
family, weddings, weeding, working on paddy fields. The
women sing more as they sashay deep into the forest: a
song on the Martian red mud of their land, on the rain
gods and another on gnomes that live in the duffs.

On days like these, during the pre-monsoon showers,
the forest often looks less promising—the wood is
already heavy with water, unseasoned. By nine in the
morning, Sukri and the others still do not have enough
for a decently sized firewood bundle on their heads. Sukri
picks up wild crop manure and berries—white, sweet
ones called *murgalhannu*, *mulaannu*, and the black ones
called *kajalaanu*. She hopes to spot, in the rain-drenched
tropical forest the iridescent bioluminescent fungus that
grows on rotting bark and twigs. Just last season, Ganga
had spotted it: 'It looks like the fireflies at night, only with

more colour.' But Sukri is never lucky. Occasionally, she plucks a few flowers of *maddale* for her husband. She will boil them in water and he'll sip on it. Her mother used to say it cured asthma. Oh, that is *brahmi*—she could fry that with onions to make his mind sharper. Roots of *kakke* and leaves of *kasamarda*—she stocks them for fever and cold. Till last year, she always took kasamarda for her children. It helped them forget the pain of dying.

By ten in the morning, Sukri's feet are blistering, so while her friends venture farther into the forest, she rests under a tree. In the transitory space before actual sleep, she has a dream: She is sitting with her back against the lighthouse, but it is nighttime, it is raining hard and there are no trees to slow the thick sheets of rain. Waves from the beach and the rain drench her, crashing down on her each time the wind gushes in. She tries to rub her hands together for some warmth, but she feels only cold fear. Despite the noisy waves, she hears nothing. The birds' cries have stopped too, she realizes, jerking awake. Sukri carefully retraces her dreams; she listens to them. People fall into trouble when they do not listen to their dreams. Putting the firewood and berries together, Sukri hurries back towards the highway. She hears a low growl, nothing like she has ever heard before. Sukri freezes, and then bolts down the path. Over the years, she has seen deer, wild boars, wild dogs and other small animals. Until a few decades ago, their men would hunt[14] for food, but after the blanket ban on hunting in 1972, that too stopped. By now, Halakki men have lost two of their major livelihoods:

hunting and slash-and-burn agriculture. All they can do is daily wage labour for landlords and higher-caste people. Some still hunted wild boars and rabbits while they gathered medicines and wood in the forests; if a tiger saw them in the forest, it usually galloped back into the thicket. But today, from the sound of its eerie, feral cry, it seems like it has lost its offspring. She thinks she sees it moving amid the faraway bushes, a shadowy animal. And then, padding across the frame, a pale tiger appears, svelte and magnificent and in no mood to spare anyone. She later sees a new carcass and hears the tiger far away, moving across the red mud outcrops, roaring at whatever might interrupt her search for her lost child.

Sukri sprints until she joins the others. At the others' surprise at seeing her sprint, she grants herself a giggle and then they all laugh together. Dark clouds are gathering in the sky overhead. The day's forest produce that she has collected will hardly bring her any money at the market; her roof has to be repaired and the moneylender she has taken a loan from for her husband's medicine will soon come knocking on her door. The last time, he had threatened to take her cow away. But that could be forgotten for now. And then, almost against their will, it seems that Sukri and her friends have made up another song. They sing about dancing so hard, about a joy so full that it cannot be held back: '*thaarley* . . .'[15]—the rain dance of the Halakkis of Ankola.

The true origin of the term 'Halakki' is possibly lost, with only verbal records of its history still available.

According to the Halakki elders, a '*holati*' or an outcast woman held control over the Konkan's coastal lands. Lord Shiva, hoping for a stronger foundation for the society, the Uttara Kannada rhetoric insists, killed the pariah woman and obtained a caste from each of her body parts, but forgot to create the Halakkis. When the 'un-created' Halakkis complained, Mahadevaraya created them from the milk and rice he was eating.[16] Another fanciful story, which is also the most vivid, is often sung by women. Lord Shiva was once ploughing fields away from their home and Parvathi, his wife, tripped and fell, along with the food she was carrying for Shiva—a pudding made of milk and rice. Parvati gathered the mess into a mound and turned it into artwork—a male and a female doll. The hungry Shiva, who was waiting for Parvathi, meanwhile, dropped his hand plough and treaded back home, keeping a look out for Parvathi in case she had lost her way to the fields. Soon, he stumbled upon the rice and milk dolls, touched them with his fingertips to see if they were real and, within minutes, with the powerful touch of the Supreme Being, they came to life. The dolls bowed and thanked him for giving them life, asking him what they could do for a living. Shiva proclaimed that since they were born while he was ploughing the field, they should continue his work. Therefore, agriculture became the main work for the shudra-caste Halakkis. A theory that stuck, however, credits the tribe's name to the rice they grow, which is white as milk: '*halu*' means milk and '*akki*' means rice. The name Halakki roughly connotes 'pure as milk and rice'.

In the beginning, Halakki Vokkaligas are said to have migrated from Andhra. Anthropologists assume this because the Halakki Vokkaligas are staunch followers of Thirupathi Thimmappa of Tirupati, Andhra Pradesh, and their songs often mention the Bay of Bengal. Their language, Achchagannada, also resembles Telugu. On their arrival on the Konkan coast, they stayed around Karwar. Like the Todas of Nilgiri, they lived near the foothills and forest borders and depended on the Kumbri[17] system of agriculture, often also hunting for a living.

When the British government debarred this slash-and-burn farming in the jungles, they gradually migrated and started living on riverbanks, the seashore and the flatlands between Honnavar and Karwar, taking up hunting, forest gathering and agriculture as their main occupations, and mixing with other communities. They participated in the Nadavas's special occasions, running small chores that were assigned to them, or in the auspicious occasions of the Havyakas, making pergolas and running other errands. They did daily wage labour for landlords when their government introduced the 'tiller is the owner'[18] scheme in the sixties and the seventies, but the paperwork was too complicated, so only a few Halakkis could claim their share of land because of lack of education and access to good lawyers.

It was in those days that Sukri's husband died. Sukri would sit in on panchayat meetings that were held under a tree farther into the village, where poor Halakki farmers talked about low yields with old seeds, complaining that they got only a small share of what they grew. An old relative once stood up and stamped his foot, exclaiming, 'We will ask the government to extend the tiller is owner law for us! We will get our lands too! We will educate our children one day!' Sukri cheered him along with others, clapping her hands, joining in the chant 'Halakki will grow too!' But she worried her people were honest and simple; too simple to understand complex politics and government systems. They thought the world around them was fair and square, hardworking and straightforward—pure like milk.

After the meetings, Sukri would continue sitting under the tree, hum a song and, slowly, other women would join in:

> *Odadeeru bandare koduvare toongula.*
> *Odedeeru alla badavaru.*
> *Bandare biduvaru maneya herikunni.*
> (When the landlord comes, they give him *toongula*, or paan.
> But the landlords are not poor.
> When the poor come, they chase them away with dogs.)

\* \* \*

Years have passed since her husband died, and Sukri still works hard in other people's fields to feed her adopted son's children. Her brother has insisted she adopt his son to fill the void that she is yet to feel.

She and the other women sow seeds in the drained paddy fields of Oomaniah. They weed the land before planting the seedlings and watch it carefully to prevent the attacks of wild animals. They work the hardest when separating the chaff from the grain using a pestle and a grinding stone; each woman works mechanically, in rhythm with the others, singing songs, breaking for lunch to eat rice wrapped in banana leaves and, in between, giggling as the fat Oomaniah waddles across, soaking his fashionable long trousers in slick, red mud.

One afternoon, when Sukri returns to the village, the sun feels like yellow fire against her skin, but it is raining. The warm drizzle mixes with her sweat and runs down in trickles on her back. There was a government rally earlier in the day and a minister had come down from Bengaluru in his convoy of Ambassadors. Flags and crumpled water pouches are strewn around an empty field along with placards that read 'Halakki will get Scheduled Tribe status'. Hundreds of Halakkis had shouted songs and joyously swayed like waves (though most of these waves were destined to never reach the shore). Somebody in the market says that men in loincloths and 'rumaals' on their heads were dancing in the rain, drunk on free bottles of *ger hand sarai* (cashew liquor) and empty promises; a throng of riled-up kids was shrieking, moving their wiry frames. The school in the village was shut; the children skipped work in fields. They are still playing *lagori* with coconut shells in the middle of the market. It is a favourite game of the Halakki children—picking up the empty shells and hurling them on to the ground, whereupon they make a satisfying crack on impact. Then a team stacks and puts the pieces together before the other team catches them all.

Sukri is taking home some stockfish today. She wonders if her adopted son and daughter-in-law, and their children, would eat real meat this week. She could not sell firewood today—the markets were shut to ensure maximum participation in the rally. With only a small bag of coins, Sukri stands before the cart of greying mackerel and imagines grabbing some, quickly tucking it into her sari folds. If she buys the mackerel, that's all she would buy. So she buys some onion, kokum and chillies to mask the meatless stockfish; if her son breaks a coconut today, they can have coconut rice with it.

Cooking is her only activity of the day that goes song-less. Singing, for Halakkis, is done for togetherness; cooking, unless it's for a wedding, is a solo activity. When her husband was alive, he loved her fish curry made with ground coconut, chillies, kokum, coriander seeds, garlic and turmeric, along with *sule* roti. However late she returned from the market, he would wait for her as she moved deliberately, slowly, smiling to herself as she saw his appetite grow with the fragrance of the ingredients. But for many years before he died, he could not swallow anything more than *ganji*—his aged limbs were thin as sticks when they cremated him.

With the stockfish bag in her hand, Sukri glances inside their hut: mattresses, cartons, sacks, clothes hanging on hooks, three clocks on the same wall. None of them works, but they display everything they own. A tasteless broth her daughter-in-law made sits in the pot, waiting for the fish.

As the curry boils, she looks outside her solitary window. Her new neighbour, a fat, widowed woman, has moved into a hut with her family. A scarecrow hangs from their pole, strung up by a piece of twine, but nobody knows why because they don't sow anything in their fields. Sukri sighs when she sees the fat woman coming towards her with a brass pot. Two days back, she had come by asking for a cup of rice. A day before, she had wanted some salt. Today, she wanted some of her fish.

'Stop giving her your food,' Vatapi, another neighbour, screams.

'At least I don't steal vegetables from other people's fields.' The woman picks a fight, dropping the brass pot on to the cow dung–smoothened floor. 'You think no one saw you plucking spinach from Gowda's fields yesterday?'

'That was wild spinach, you fool. Go to the forest and fields and work. You're not a Halakki if you are begging another poor person.'

Work, for the Halakkis, is a way of life; they never resort to begging even if they are totally helpless. Halakkis use the home only to rest after a hard day's work; home, for them, is not a place to spend time being lazy. They call their homes '*bidara*' or camp, indicating the informal temporariness of the place.

Yet, her adopted son lies all day where her husband used to lie, drunk on nausagara, a cashew liquor with jaggery and some potent fertilizer for increased intoxication, destroyed by the loss of his own sense of self. Sukri feels a surge of revulsion, the urge to run and run and run till she is at the lighthouse from her childhood.

In the evenings, when Sukri is milking her cow, her daughter-in-law's voice tears across the banana and coconut trees and beyond the holy basil altar, down to the cowshed.

'You neutered goat, don't you dare ask me for money,' she fights with her husband. 'My children need to go to school and you lie there all day. Why don't you kill yourself instead of drinking this slow poison every night?' she cries.

In the shed, Sukri sings to her cow, '*Bith danna vedeko* (you reap as you sow) . . .'

A few girls from the neighbourhood listen while making flat pancakes with cow dung to use as fuel for the kitchen stove.

'Why do we sing to the cow, *ajji*?'[19] the girls ask.

'They milk better when you sing to them.'

'But why are you teaching it? Cows cannot learn.'

'Cows, unlike you girls, don't like running around too much. They prefer sitting in a corner and thinking quietly. Come, see it in their intelligent eyes, behind those thick lashes.'

Sukri comes from a world where women keep their husbands' and sons' secrets; when they don't, they cannot count on police for protection. Women here don't read books; they don't save money or food for themselves or leave home in the night, let alone travel to other cities. So when Boralingaiah came knocking on her door one day, the boat in which she would travel the world had arrived.

\* \* \*

One day, when she came back from the fields, she found at her doorstep H.C. Boralingaiah, a folk expert and former vice chancellor of Kannada University at Hampi. Every time he visited Badageri, he was left astounded at the chain of songs Halakki women left behind everywhere they went.

'Who knows the most songs here?' Boralingaiah asked the villagers, and found himself knocking Sukri's door. He was amused by her sudden gestures and spontaneity, which seemed childlike.

'How many songs can you sing? he asked her.

'We can sing many. How many do you need?'

He cackled. Sukri was not sure what was funny, but she smiled in return.

'Only women sing these songs? No men?' Boralingaiah asked.

When he expressed surprise, Sukri thought about why men don't sing enough folk songs. They played gumte[20] and sang during festivals, but when women are singing through the day, the men are always in some other place, lazing, drinking, wagering, labouring or dying.

Boralingaiah put Sukri and her friends, who often sang with her while working, on a bus to Dharwad.[21] Like on the days of the Suggi festival, they took a bath with soapnut, wore their best saris, tied traditionally with a thread on to one shoulder, finishing with flowers in their bun. It was a hot summer afternoon and the bus drove at a crawl through the thick crowds. At the bus station in Dharwad, women put baskets of produce on their heads with babies tied to their fronts; men carried chickens, plastic bags and cartons, hoping to make fortunes elsewhere. Men, women, children were all drenched with sticky, sweaty hope.

In Dharwad, they met Bananduru Kempaiah of the Dharwad radio station Akashvani Kendra. They recorded them after several attempts, and Sukri was surprised how croaky her voice sounded as it echoed back, unlike the honey-smoothness of the early morning programme conductor on the radio. But her songs sound like what they are: endangered indigenous songs that narrate life, songs that talk of sexual relationships between the husband's brother and his wife (permissible until a few decades ago), fantasies of men stroking their wives with flowers that grow in a lake near Tirupati, sexual imagery of the woman who comes into the family to bear children and continue the family lineage, and then their natural surroundings, the water they drink, forests, fields, rocks and the animals they have as playmates. Halakkis hardly camouflage their sexual desires, speaking of breasts and homes in the same way they would speak about a complex emotion, with dazzling abandon, not the usual western meticulousness or spare watchfulness. What is arresting about Sukri's usage of the lyrics is that there is no segregation between the everyday and the exotic.

She was completely taken aback when the men applauded their singing. But she knew this applause shouldn't be for her. She clarified, 'Most of the pretty songs and clever lyrics are my ancestors'—my mother's, my aunt's and my grandmother's. The way my mother could

sing a song about a fretful child or spring winds . . .' Sukri
stopped. The cultured, educated men outside the recording
room, with oiled hair and starched kurtas, were looking
at her woodenly. Nagge Gowda, head of Janpada Loka, a
museum an hour away from Bengaluru that housed and
celebrated indigenous local culture, was among them. He
politely asked her to perform at Janpada, quickly following
it with a request to wear the modern sari with a blouse to
appear more cultured.

Sukri flatly refused to wear it.

In the years to come, they were invited to folk festivals
and performances all over Karnataka. Sukri's songs celebrate
the Halakkis's adoration of their art and the primeval nature
of their land, her disgust at the exploitative nature of men
and women, her eagerness to understand the beginning of
this world and to find some hope for the future.

In one of their popular songs, Halakkis give a version of
the origin of life and earth. The story goes like this: When
there was nothing in the universe, there appeared a bird
called *anjuga*. The bird laid some eggs. One of the eggs was
broken and the contents formed the universe. The water in
the egg became the sea, the white portion became the sky
and the remaining solid matter became the earth.

Govind Mahalay, a barber who also worked with
Akashvani,[22] took them to Bengaluru. None of them had
been on a Volvo bus before. For a long time, Sukri thought
she would freeze into stone if she fell asleep, despairing of
ever reaching Bengaluru. Men and women stared at her;
girls asked her where she bought her magnificent beads

from. In Bengaluru, Sukri went to the top of a windy sixteen-floor building. Soft flute-like music played from an unknown device and the cool breeze was fragranced with sweet-scented flowers—at that moment, she wondered if this was the Indraloka from her songs.[23]

From an auto, they saw the great actor and singer Rajkumar's house, and Sukri knew they'd be singing about this moment on her front porch in her village the next evening. Govind showed her Chief Minister Ramakrishna Hegde's house; she sat before its gate and bowed her head. Later that evening, she performed at a hall before dignitaries and hundreds of people at a state function. They waited in the gardens outside the hall for their turn at the food, eating the cold sambar with overcooked rice served to them; the clean corner was nothing like the green the children in her village love to play in with its bosky boundaries, climbable trees and shady corners to lie under on hot sunny days; one could sniff the fennel, *indrani* and *haritake* that grow alongside bananas, chillies and spinach behind the village homes. A trimmed tree would never bear fruits; she clicked her tongue. A tree that was revered in her village was used only as an ornament here.

Inside the hall, thickly garlanded dignitaries on the stage spoke with frequent pauses—and not because thunderous applause kept interrupting them. There was no thunderous applause. The audience's eyes had long since glazed over from the tedium. A group of musicians asked Sukri if they should play background music to support her vocals, but she dismissed the idea with a wave of her hand: 'It'll just be noise.'

Soon, she took the stage with other women from her village and stood before hundreds. Just over five feet tall, with bare, bent shoulders and knuckles swollen out of her toes from her daily uphill walks, Sukri is hailed as the singing woman of Ankola. Her paan-stained mouth, at rest, has a melancholic air, but a ready smile lights it up. As the mic was adjusted, she drank water from a plastic bottle. Most of it dripped down her throat and she wiped it the back of her hand. She stood like a dancer, with one toe pointed out, hip jutting out and then suddenly broke into song, with the others following her lead. The songs were rhythmic, nearly mesmeric, but never featured percussion, instead alternating between speech and song. Despite the absence of accompanying music, her jingles swallowed the hall up. She was metamorphic.

Many stood up clapping, and Sukri continued singing the last song while feeling the warm glow of pride spread up from the tips of her toes. When she finished, a man came up on to the stage, saying many words of encouragement, and touched her feet. Later, she learnt that it was actor Rajkumar's son. Since then, Sukri always washes her feet and leaves her dusty chappals behind before getting on to any stage.

* * *

Removing chappals, though, is not allowed in Delhi. It wasn't her first time to the capital, but her first time in an airplane, years after her first train trip to Bengaluru. After a frightful journey in the clouds, she found herself at the Rashtrapati Bhavan, practising walking up to a chair and sitting back. They said she would be awarded the Padma Shri by a certain 'President', the country's supreme head—like Shiva. There were cauliflower-haired old men and women with teeth like neatly arranged boxes who ate with spoons she had never learnt to hold. She longed to be back at the Rajyostav award ceremony in Karnataka, where they served rice and curry on banana leaves. The then chief minister, J.H. Patel, had awarded her 1,00,000 rupees, with which she would build her dream two-storey pukka 'manne'. The Padma Shri, they said, would get her honour but no money.

Sukri was still in Delhi after the award function, gazing at the starless sky, when she received the news of her adopted son's death. Her knees gave way; she sank to the floor in the government guest house, her back hunched, her shoulders sagging, feeling faint. Her grandson had only just started school. They had no field and she was too old to work in other people's fields. She would have to sell the gold earrings she had bought for her daughter-in-law in exchange for the next few months of ration. The friend who had accompanied her to Delhi told her to stop crying, but she did not really mean it. Sukri dislodged years of grief, the passing away of everyone she knew—her mother, father, husband, little children and a grown-up son. Years had crawled past worrying about her son; that he would float away in the river, drunk; that something would happen to him and nobody would know where to find his family. As tears poured down her cheeks and soaked her sari, she felt an odd sense of relief: that she wouldn't have to worry about him anymore. The only pleasure she got from finally living with a son was outliving him.

Her friend broke into her thoughts: 'Your son's funeral money?'

\* \* \*

Days after returning from Delhi, Sukri was sitting on her porch, drying some groundnut, while her daughter-in-law was away in the fields. Kusuma Sorab, a Western medicine doctor who helped women with health issues, was going around the village with a loudspeaker. The doctor was urging the Badageri gramsabha and the villagers to ban spurious liquor. Kusuma akka had started an agitation with the women who were left to fend for themselves when unlicensed liquor shops—a constant menace in the villages along the north Karnataka coast—snatched away the lives of the men in their family.

'But how else must we release our pain?' a young man asked Kusuma akka. If he did not drink, the worry of interest to be paid on the loan he had taken for his mother's funeral would kill him. 'The spurious liquor keeps us going. If you ban it, how will we afford the stuff from the shop?'

'You must work, you wretch. Go farm your own vegetables and help your woman in the forest,' an old grandmother replied.

'Farm a rented plot? You talk, but try being a man, you wrinkled, old hag. I lost all my good seed in the drought last year and if I buy a new bag, I'll have to take another loan. I might as well give up on that land and buy more liquor.'

'And then beat up your wife! You lousy man with no spine,' the old woman spat on the floor beside her. 'In our times, hard-working women were given more respect in the Karwar region than men. Now, these useless men have started imitating those higher-class people, eating into our ways of being.'

After a tense pause, Kusuma akka asked the old woman, 'Why do you allow yourselves to be shut up by these men?'

'Men are stronger than women,' someone murmured.

Kusuma akka smiled. 'Even a wild boar is stronger than a man. How come you eat him before he eats you?'

Here was someone who finally spoke about issues and people, unlike at the big award functions where people only spoke about themselves, Sukri thought. She listened to the sabha with rapt attention. Most men around them were loafers, nincompoops, and—with a doubt—alcoholics. Women did not only their share of work but, for most part, also accepted this as their fate. The only man left in her family, her grandson, must be spared this fate. He must learn to study and work hard, not use alcohol as an excuse, Sukri decided.

The next time Kusuma akka spoke in Sirsi, a village close to theirs, Sukri planted herself on stage, in front of the record player, and supported Kusuma akka's speech with her improvised gumte songs, which were usually sung by men. When Kusuma akka's team member tried to remove her, the doctor intervened: 'Leave her be, she is a good woman.' Sukri folded her hands in gratitude. When the show ended, Kusuma akka folded her hands at Sukri too.

In the coming months, Sukri joined Kusuma akka and sang against the ban on spurious liquor. They travelled and spoke at the gramsabhas all over Uttara Karnataka: Siddapura, Sirsi, Benegowi, Belgaum, Karwar. Her thick, deep octogenarian's voice was a bit shaky, but still resonant with ideas and beliefs. These were songs of the struggle of women, she announced, and when you sang them, they spread the revolutionary message.

Sukri's audience in the villages still does not understand the relevance of her songs, of the Halakki traditions or of Sukri's Padma Shri. Often, the songs she sings are dismissed by the villagers with mere applause and an occasional honour, but every once in a while, when their distant and distinct ideologies meet, the resulting vibrations produce something unanticipated and magnificent.

# 2

## THE KANJARS OF CHAMBAL

*A former dacoit whose fathers and grandfathers have been known to survive on lizards in jungles*

Jhalrapatan, Rajasthan

That night, there was a serene calm in this village square in Rajasthan, in the gentle wave of the babul trees and the citrus fragrance of the ripening oranges around it. It belied what happened later. In the pearly light, not of the moon but of silence and emptiness, a group of men came into the village with knives, lathis and rusty old razors. They drugged the poor street dogs to sleep, finished their work and left. Before dawn, half a dozen groggy dogs stumbled to the square and howled together to rouse the villagers, making sure their grievances were heard.

Seconds later, women jerked open their doors.

'My home has been looted,' one of them cried beneath her veil, beating her chest; a glass bangle or two broke into her skin.

'*Ae mata rani*, all my gold is gone. They even pulled out my earrings while I lay sleeping,' shrieked another. 'My daughters' wedding . . .' she wailed.

Another threw herself near the body of her husband and rolled around in the dirt, crying, 'Oh God, why my husband? Why him; he was a good man.' She had found him knocked dead near the well with a fatal injury on his head; he was probably chasing the looters. A few women gathered around and helped her up. The men of the village, who, though men, had no mettle, only smoked their chillum long and slow.

Later in the evening, at the police station, the sarpanch of the village and a few other men stood before the havaldar. Gauging the moment, the sarpanch asked the havaldar if he might say a word; the havaldar nodded along, never looking up from the potato-stuffed kachoris.

'Sahib,[1] as you know,' said the sarpanch, folding his hands before the havaldar, 'this police station governs the land from here to the Kalsindh river, and there is no village as peaceful as ours. We barely fill our stomachs,' here the sarpanch stroked his paunch with a paw, 'and yet, we don't cause trouble to anyone.' The police havaldar licked the chutney off his fingers and then he scrunched up his brows, recalling the complaint of a sower who had been whipped by this sarpanch on his fields for being slow. 'Enough, sir, enough.' The sarpanch shook his head and squeezed his eyes shut. 'I hesitate, but my mouth speaks . . . the gold jewellery, the radio sets were all the meagre savings of our villagers. The man whom they killed was the sole breadwinner in his family. These robbers must be found and hanged!'

The havaldar was familiar with these loot-and-kill stories, though they were not usually this elaborate; he listened to the sarpanch while making paper planes from the oily newspapers the kachoris came in. Nodding patiently, he placed the planes in a row according to size, waiting for the honking outside the station to stop.

'Did you see anyone new around the village?'

'Two women had arrived the day before, my wife had told me,' an ordinary man in a white dhoti standing behind the sarpanch spoke up meekly. 'With cloth bundles on their heads and babies on their waists.' '*Asli gota zari sari!*' the women had chanted, walking the baulks between irrigated fields of sugarcane and soya—verdant and luscious in this particular village despite the scorching sun. Late afternoon had always been a good time for the women to hawk their wares, when the wives were just back from the wells, the children were playing marbles in dust near the coops, the girls were hiding in the barns and tall fields, and the men were not back yet from their day jobs at the thakurs' homes or in the fields or wherever else they liked to pretend to be when they were outside home. The women ushered them in; 'no tea, no tea,' the sellers waved away the steaming cups as the village women lusted after the yards and yards of glittering, embellished fabrics they unfolded in their rooms at compelling prices. But the wives haggled nevertheless, eager to tell their neighbours about the steal deals.

The sellers had arresting eyes—grey-green against their burnt, brown skin—the sort that trap you if you look too long. But that's all the wives could tell about the faces, for they were visible for only a few moments before the sellers adjusted the long veils covering their faces. Beneath the veils, though, their eyes were like hoverflies, nectaring about the home or canvassing the villages before choosing their husbands' targets for looting later. Within minutes, they had absorbed images from the village like a movie—the turns they took on the streets, the thickness of the jewellery the women wore; covert back doors; loose floor tiles; trunks that were stashed in the attics. They sought particular homes that seemed to be busy with a wedding or other festivities and lax about security. Or just places that attracted them, where something was waiting for them in the end.

'This sounds like the work of Kanjars, the invisible dacoits! They are known to run very fast, disappearing into the jungles and crossing over state borders. File a complaint,' the havaldar told the sarpanch and other men of the village '. . . but don't expect much. You made it easy for them. No one saw the men or heard them come and leave; they left no clues. Beat your wives for letting those Kanjari women in!'

\* \* \*

'*Kanjaron ki tarah mat karo* (don't act like Kanjars)!' mothers tell their ill-behaved children in this region. By that, they mean vulgar, uncivilized behaviour. Seemingly excluded from proper society, in practice, dacoits have always occupied some of its deepest domains in the Indian subcontinent since pre-historic times. Ancient Indian literature by the likes of Bhasa, Dandin and Somadeva describes these thieving communities as a specific caste, different from other castes.[2] Robbers in Dandi's *Dasakumaracharita* dwelt in moonless night, underground lairs and the jungles—the perennial fringe of South Asian societies.[3] The ancient text *Manusmriti*[4] says that theft itself is the art of 'deception and disguise' and professional robbers or the *aprakasataskara*[5] are 'invisible' people.

Kanjar is not a caste, but a general term used for forest vagabonds (derived from the word 'kan-kachar': one who wanders in the jungle). The caste Bhatus, which we document in this story, meanwhile, of which a few people came to be known as Kanjars, was once a community of valorous Rajputs fighting for kings and their kingdoms' safety; soon, they were pushed to the fringes of the society by multiple invaders in the Indian subcontinent. The unquestionably ferocious Alauddin Khilji, in the early 1300s, laid siege to the fort of Chittorgarh in a quest to gain control over the Mewar region.[6] Upon victory, he ordered a wide-ranging massacre of Chittor's population. According to Amir Khusrau, the historian who accompanied Khilji, 30,000 Hindus were 'cut down like dry grass', while many of the erstwhile king's soldiers, the Bhati Rajputs,[7] fled into the jungles or hid in the immense ravines intersecting the Chambal river, styling themselves as *baghis* or rebels, outside the regular Rajput order of politeness. Waves of Rajput refugees sought asylum in these Chambal *bihads*. The soldiers seem to have wandered all over Rajasthan, Madhya Pradesh, Uttar Pradesh and Punjab, enduring many vicissitudes for over two centuries.

In the course of time, many such soldiers fleeing from outsiders' attacks, settled back into the villages,[8] acquired land, status and influence, and even raised kingdoms after being absorbed into local communities and adopting indigenous caste names. Those who lived in the jungles,

meanwhile, became dacoits who also sheltered political
fugitives, rebels and outlaws. They have since operated out
of those jungles. Robbery was their means of subsistence,
and terrorism, their modus operandi. Although they
were spared the dire fate of the 'untouchables', they still
remained on the fringes, living away from villages and
attracting into their ranks the outcasts and the frustrated
of every passing epoch.

Hoonkar Singh Patel is one of these 'invisible' persons.
On his first dacoity, perhaps in the early sixties, he had
arrived in a village along the border of Rajasthan and
Madhya Pradesh, just off the scrubby and thorny forests
of the Chambal ravines. With his brothers and uncles,
Hoonkar walked into this newly affluent village of traders.
His heart hammering, he sketched out fatal scenarios as
he thought about how he might be 'encountered': a police
sahib might catch him, put him behind bars, give him a
bag of laddoos on an empty stomach and then deprive him
of water; he could be frisked by police on his way out of
the village and shot in the groin, dying of pain; or he might
get separated from his brothers while being chased and be
eaten by a wild animal. His older cousin shook him out of
his reverie when a police jeep patrolled up the street. While
others hurried to hide behind bushes, the cousin found
them both a trench.

Hoonkar lay still for many damp uncomfortable
minutes inside the trench as a worm clambered up his arm,
surprised to find not cold underground earth, but warm
human flesh. It was a moonless, windy night; Hoonkar

hoped for a little quiet so that he could hear the former zamindar's guards finally snooze and snore. Nature had been more generous when they had left their camp hours ago; now, the wind was brooding, crying through the trees. After what felt like an hour, the cousin swore under his breath, '*Dina ki sou*,[9] I'll kill this *durban* if he doesn't fall asleep.'

The Kanjars generally worked in a group, scrambling up walls, hopping between rooftops and picking locks. When a mynah called out in the middle of the night, Hoonkar knew it was their uncle's signal: the path was clear. The watchman had disappeared into a room with a housemaid; he made low moaning sounds while his uncle soundlessly dug a hole through the mud wall of the house with an iron rod they carried with them. This process required special techniques; one of them was torturing a dog so that it yelped loudly and the digging went unheard.

Within minutes, the youngest of the gang, Hoonkar, was jostled in through the hole to open the house door for the rest of his gang. In villages, the men slept outside on the porch in the summers, which made it easier for Hoonkar's gang to pull necklaces and earrings off the sleeping women without so much as stirring them. Once inside the house, they stealthily looked for money, and then jewellery, because it was valuable and easy to sell. A burglary that took less than two hours often yielded enough cash to support their entire gang for a fortnight.

Hoonkar was admiring the pearls and gold hidden in a tin jar in the kitchen when a young man appeared in the room, rubbing sleep out of his eyes. For the briefest moment, Hoonkar's intestines clenched with fear. What if he couldn't hit him right? What if he injured his legs, an act forbidden among the Kanjars who had high moral principles like their warrior ancestors—the Rajputs? What if he screamed and the entire gang was caught? But then he struck his lathi, just like his uncle had taught him to—'Hit them just above the neck,' he'd said, 'to strike them down with a single blow'. This was how they killed the goats and the pigs that they stole from the farms. From the other room, he could hear his uncle kill someone else—a woman, he guessed, from the sound of her bangles crashing on to the floor.

'Strip him! Take his clothes!' someone whispered in their argot, as Hoonkar put the young man on the ground. The Kanjars spoke many argots, or secret tongues. This 'apas ki boli', which others could not comprehend, was almost instinctive, acquired by being born and raised in the community.

'Pockets only! We don't have time,' another voice said.

Hoonkar leaned over the body; in the chest pocket, he felt some cash, a ring and warm, thick blood. Suddenly, the dead man seemed to stir, and Hoonkar shivered.

'Let's go!' his cousin whispered, tugging at Hoonkar as he wiped his blooded hands on his kurta. They ran till they reached the roads and their jootis echoed on the highway.

Well away from the village, his uncles and brothers thumped his back: 'You have blood on your hands. A big man, hain . . .' Hoonkar longed to wash off the stickiness of the blood but success slowly lifted his spirits, even as the dead man's open eyes flashed before him; he floated through the next few hours, drinking liquor from a bottle that they carried with them. His cousin rolled up some dried leaves and they all smoked together, not bothering to hide their drinks and smokes in their blankets since their uncle was happy.

They forced open a highway dhaba, ate mutton kebabs and rolled some more crisp leaves into a smoke. When the owner asked for payment, his uncle shook the wimpy man by his collar. 'My dear man,' his uncle grated out from between his teeth, posing as a policeman, 'I'll handcuff you, lock you up in prison and make you look like a robber.' While the man apologetically yelped, 'Sorry sahib, sorry sahib,' Hoonkar laughed. When he laughed, it was clear that his voice had not cracked yet. Among the five men, he looked small, not yet an adolescent. He was just twelve.

\* \* \*

By the end of that winter, Hoonkar had already been on three or four heists; his confidence as a burglar grew to the point that he felt 'indestructible and invulnerable'. Once, while fleeing from the police across the rooftops of a village off Jhalrapatan, he went down the staircase to find himself in the middle of a *baraadari*[10] or a courtesans' pavilion, dimly lit with colourful lights, Shakila's 'Babuji dheere chalna' playing somewhere in the background. Two women, red with rage, were beating a man with their heeled footwear in the pavilion.

'*Haramzade*,[11] no money, you say? You think this is a dharamshala?' they screamed.

Another woman, heavily made up and wearing fake gold and a dazzling orange ghaghra, laughed as she watched the man whimpering from the balcony. Suddenly, she turned around and noticed Hoonkar. Raising a sardonic eyebrow, she sashayed to him, took in his large eyes, dirty kurta pyjama and then, to Hoonkar's mortification, pulled his cheeks.

'This is no place to be in for a sweet little boy,' she murmured. Hoonkar was too mesmerized by her unearthly glow to respond.

'How did you get here? Oh, look at you . . .' She ruffled his hair, and without waiting for a reply from him, held his hand and took him to her room, giving him a cold roti with pickle. 'I'm Lali. Single and happy,' she introduced herself, and lounged on the bed as she told her life story. 'No one in this baraadari marries, my boy, except, occasionally, to an odd prince,' she told him. 'You don't look much of a prince, so hard luck.' She threw her head back and laughed, revealing a long, smooth neck. 'Oh, but many here love women too. It is called *chapat bazi*,' she whispered.

'I have tried but have not been pregnant yet. My lover, this rich trader who now lives in Pakistan, abandoned me; I was hoping to have a child with him so that we could run away, get married, but alas, I'm barren. But I'm also rich.' She cackled with laughter. 'And far better off than many lovers whom I have so blithely ruined.'

Hoonkar slept beside her bed that night, on the floor, constantly patting the stolen jewels in his inner chest pocket to reassure and perhaps to remind himself of who he really was, and where he ought to be. Around midnight, when everything was quiet in the alleys outside, Hoonkar tiptoed out of the room, but not before casting a last glance at the lady on the bed. He was first drawn to her bottom lip, and the two small folds on both the sides of it, and then, because she was lying down, he tilted his head so that he could look at her face directly. She looked ethereal without the ornaments—raw, full and very beautiful. And even though it was very dark outside, her face had lit up, scorched and then melted right before his eyes. It was a relief when she eventually turned away, covering her face with her blanket; he closed the door on her, walking back to where he belonged.

It was daybreak by the time Hoonkar found himself trudging along the ravines of Chambal. There were no fields, homes or outposts in this area of Chambal; all he could see was the sun pulsing off the dark rocks, so that sharp edges seemed to be embedded with knives. Halfway through the bihads, Hoonkar met two members of his gang: his cousin and another boy, who had waited for him there all night.

'We knew you'd be alive,' they said and jumped up, forcing him into a hug.

'Where did you spend the night?'

Hoonkar hesitantly told them about his adventure: the baraadari, the dances, the women curling up in the laps of men, and Lali.

'Oh, Lali! That Lali! They say that her oscillating hips,' the boys demonstrated, swinging their hips from side to side, 'can send men to reveries of infidelity.' They slapped his back, laughed, and pressed him for more details as they trudged towards the jungle.

Hoonkar faked indifference in front of his fellows. He wanted to appear manly, as if a beautiful woman barely titillated him. To their oohs and aahs, he coolly told them about the jasmine in her hair and her bed that was covered in the softest silk. The bumpkins stared at him agog, salivating slightly. But he did not tell them about the drunk men who came to those women all night. Hoonkar thought about the dangerous nights ahead of Lali with those slobbery policemen who forced themselves into their rooms; he could have slipped one of the stolen gold jewels under her pillow. Or he could have left all of it for her and made up a story for the gang.

Hoonkar almost said something about it to the boys, but he knew what they would say; feeding themselves and their families first was all they had ever learnt in the jungles. He turned often to look at her village as its roofs disappeared into the horizon. Alongside the dirt path that they walked on, Kalsindh, a tributary of the river Chambal, flowed by, shallow and clear water over a bed of stones. Hoonkar longed to go back to Lali and see her beautiful face. But what would he tell her? Who was he? A dacoit? Even courtesans were afraid of dacoits. Hoonkar sighed and watched the mayflies appear in the hundreds, with eager small fish leaping agape for them and dunking back in. Long-billed vultures and wary hyenas emerged from behind the trees, stretching themselves and stopping for a drink; the gentle upheavals on the water's skin had revealed the predatory profiles of the surfacing gharials. Dark myths in ancient Indian texts, Hoonkar knew, referred to this river as Charmanyavati, originating from the blood of thousands of cows sacrificed by the Aryan king Rantidev and thus considered 'unholy' in Hindu tradition.[12] This stark landscape, he mused, is what must have built the character of the dacoits.

The Kanjar Bhatus were resilient and resolutely autonomous, escaping both state and local panchayats. Every few months, their *giroh*, a miniature fiefdom consisting mostly of a bunch of extended families, would carry with them bundles and boxes on their heads, chickens and rolled up mats under their arms their only possessions. They always knew where they were going through the charted, dangerous paths into the jungles; they walked briskly, at the same pace, and often more than thirty miles in one night.

In the *sikris*—tents made of sticks and the narkel plant that moved with the Kanjars from camp to camp—life was tough. Erected in the ravines within the shrubbery to avoid detection, the sikris, where five people would sleep, had only space for two. Wilds cats and foxes idled around them in the night; mattresses crawled with bed bugs and the wheat they stole quickly got infested with weevils. Kanjar women would preserve the vegetables by drying them and cook them over pits early in the mornings, before dawn, to avoid the camps being detected. On the days they anticipated raids, the women would not cook.

In these jungle camps of ten to twelve huts, together known as the giroh, hunger was a constant state, a habit formed in childhood and blunted by smoking hash or brewing homemade alcohol. So for lunch on such days, Hoonkar and his cousin would climb the *ber* trees and munch on the fruits, annoying the girls by flinging the seeds at them; for dinner, they would smoke chillum on nearly empty stomachs, hiding under the blankets and choking on their own smoke, or fill themselves up with *kaccha khatiya*,[13] an illicit liquor they made in large batches from sugarcane juice in the nights. The Kanjar Bhatus were good at doing things in the night; their eyes were trained to see in the dark.

Once, during the monsoons, their giroh was cut off for months by the rain-fed Kalsindh river. That season, three weeks went by and the giroh was still surviving on potatoes and onions. And then one day, someone returned with a sickly goat on their shoulder, its legs tied together; it was so thin that one could count its ribs. Its ankles had been tied together with rope to keep it from running away. Bleating meekly, it scarcely chewed on bramble bush. Next morning, the men gathered together, excited at the thought of meat. Two of them killed it and made a fire. It is said that they ate even its bones.

On the days Hoonkar was not stealing, his life would feel as purposeless as that of a housefly: swinging from the trees, moseying on the fringes of a village stealing chickens, playing on rail tracks, pocketing soft bread from vendors on bicycles or learning new smoking tricks—making rings, emitting smoke from nose and ears.

In the evenings, the boys and men of the giroh would huddle in one of the sikris, open bottles of kaccha khatiya and narrate to each other instances of their community's bravado. They listened to stories of the time when their ancestors kidnapped the British for amusement, and to add piquancy, kill them and send them back home on their horses. And then would come the stories of the valorous, famed Sultana Daku, who had once pillaged half of a village and murdered fifteen people simply to impress upon the village the measure of retribution that collaboration with the police could attract. However, no one ever spoke about his capture near Nainital by a Britisher, Freddy Young, and the ultimate death at the gallows. The men rarely spoke of weaknesses or failures; it was better to leave each man's load unopened, undisturbed, in his own heart.

'And that time, when Chand Singh here,' one of the old men would say, patting the shoulder of Hoonkar's moustachioed uncle, 'cut off the nose of a police constable to avenge the death of his courageous brother Lala, this boy's father . . .', he said, and everyone proudly turned to Hoonkar.

Back in 1871, the newly formed colonial government in India decided to enact a piece of legislation known as the 'Criminal Tribe Act', which declared a large number of communities in India as 'criminal tribes', defined as 'a tribe whose ancestors were criminals, who are themselves destined by the usages of caste (system of India) to commit crime and whose descendants will be offenders against law, until the whole tribe is exterminated or accounted for in the manner of the Thugs'.[14]

And the rubric was cast wide:

'If the local government has the reason to believe that any tribe, gang, or class of person is addicted to the systematic commission of non-bailable offences, it may report to the Governor-General in council, and may request his permission to declare such tribe, gang or class a criminal one.'

The Governor General was vested with wide-ranging authority to declare practically any community a criminal tribe, even if they were just a group or a gang, not a tribe. So how did, in one stroke, the colonial masters invent a new category?

Two gentlemen of the colonial era, Medows Taylor and Captain Sleeman, between them, triggered a sequence of events that led to the formation of the Act of Thugee in 1830, and the more elaborate Criminal Tribes Act of 1871. Taylor, neither nobility nor erudite, arrived in India, green and willing and raring to prove himself. Serving the Nizam of Hyderabad, cosy in the Shorapur fort, he wrote the *Confessions of a Thug*—deemed as good as his fictional accounts of India—with people as beautiful and stark as he wished to see in his descriptions. The book caught Queen Victoria's fancy; it was lauded, questionably, as rich 'ethnographic material' and marked the discovery of the thugs by the colonialists. Captain Sleeman, the pioneer of the 'eradication of thugee', soon followed it with voluminous accounts of the secret society of thugs,[15] and later, shifted his attention to newly discovered 'fraternities of hereditary robbers', expressing moral horror and avowing to 'finish the menace'. He famously claimed at a gathering in Madras, ' . . . if you have a very sweet dog that bites children, you have to choose the children, and put the dog down.'

Hoonkar's father, Lala Singh, was one such dog.

Lala was an exceptional robber; he often returned to plush homes without stealing anything, so that he could admire the exquisite pieces they housed. It thrilled him to be within hand's reach of beautiful art and craft in the homes that he stole from. A gentleman dacoit, when he stole, he hardly ever left a house in a mess and always killed people in one stroke, with minimal blood spilled. His old, rundown sikri had a carved wooden elephant, a jade necklace and silver coins from faraway countries.

Lala was married early in life to Asan bai, a girl his parents had chosen, a woman of unsurpassed fertility. It was a virtue that was tested, as a popular Kanjar ritual, on the first night of their marriage. The women removed the bride's jewellery and any sharp objects from the tent and then the groom was sent inside with white sheets.

While the marriage was being consummated in one of the tarpaulin tents, the elders stood outside.

When Lala, the 'boy-turned-man', emerged from the tent, 'How was the *maal* (the goods)?' his grandfather asked. 'Was the glass broken?'

To everyone's joy and relief, there was blood on the sheets, a suggestion that the hymen was not broken before tonight due to previous sexual intercourse. If the groom did not confirm three times that his wife was a virgin, the elders would announce a punishment which could entail beatings for the bride, monetary penalty and, often, the end of the marriage. Lala's cousin, who was married just months before them, had had no blood on her sheet. They refused to believe that her hymen could have been ruptured out of natural causes; her grandfather, uncles and father had rushed to her in-laws' giroh to burn her alive and dissolve the body in acid, to be sure they had erased the family's shame.

The virtuous Asan bai, meanwhile, quickly proceeded to bear children for Lala. Every year, if not every nine months, she reproduced, and all daughters, one after another after another; until after four daughters, finally, the much looked-for son, Hoonkar, arrived.

'*Janeman,*' Lala would address his wife, standing at the entrance of their sikri, where she'd be sitting on her haunches, picking lice from one of their daughters' hair. She'd quickly cover her head with her veil on seeing him, pushing her daughter out to attend to her husband's need.

'What is cooking for me?' he'd ask her suggestively, with a handsome, lopsided smile, and as she rushed out with a plate to bring him food, he would stand at the entrance to the sikri, squeezing her bottom as she went past.

Asan bai, despite having borne five children, had a lithe, strong body; she was light-skinned with grey-green eyes. A lost vagrant whom they once gave shelter to in their giroh, asked her if she was terrified her husband wouldn't return one day. She said she wasn't. Lala chuckled when he overheard the conversation. 'I look like the *sur*, the pig, but if you want to rob a well-guarded angrez officer's home, she's the one to do it,' he had said.

She hid with him in jungles where scorpions and snakes crawled into their tents; often working out of bunkers beneath their homes where they hid all the loot. After Hoonkar and his gang looted the jewellery, she wore it and took another direction back home. At times, she acted as a messenger between fugitives, passing along tiny, folded notes. She played the role of a paymaster and bookkeeper, distributing the loot among families depending on their need, skills or their husbands' contribution to the robbery.

Once, in a meeting, their gang discussed the death of a member who was killed by the villagers. The men proposed killing the sarpanch. Then Asan bai spoke up from behind her veil. 'Kill them *all*,' she'd said. 'Even the women. And the children.'

In his last years, Lala would frequently get his gang members to their sikri, asking for tea or kebabs. As if the delay would mean an expression of dissent, she would not blow on the wood to quicken the heating. And when Lala would see her sitting idle before the fire, he would beat her up.

Apart from on one or two occasions, Lala did not abuse her. He spat at her, shoved her, and tried to break everything in their sikri. He didn't dispute with his cousins that it happened, but as long as it wasn't the face, they didn't see it as hitting.

Lala Singh was bright, resourceful and daring. When he moved with his commune from jungle to jungle, he was always in disguise. He had a collection of fake noses and teeth; when police or villagers caught up with him, he'd disappear into the bushes and step out in a demure ghaghra, with bottles of spiked kaccha khatiya. Lala was made of fallacies and ferocity and, above all, of ego. Under his leadership, hundreds of homes were looted by his giroh; many travellers stripped bare of their tiniest belongings. More than often, he distributed the extras among the poor villages close to the giroh. A master of his lathi, he was also fast with his fists, always ready to pummel people to unconsciousness or death. In a gory retelling, a whole family from his giroh was once put to death for leaking his whereabouts to the police. More than once, Lala and his giroh were surrounded by the police, but the wily old fox managed to evade his pursuers. He could charm the skin off a snake, apparently. This was most likely apocryphal. However, it was perhaps the confidence that he could do so that served Lala so well in his sordid life.

It was also this confidence that ultimately took him down.

This was just years after the Indian independence, when Lala's giroh was stationed deep in the jungles of Harnavadha, Rajasthan, among leopards and panthers. That spring, angrez officers seemed to be everywhere, monitoring the exit of the British from the country, while Indian police officers too joined the troupe. It was getting hard to loot homes and Lala was restless, sitting idle in the jungles.

Dado, a homeless soothsayer, had been living with their giroh as long as there had been trees in the jungle. He had once predicted a smashing loot for one of the grandfathers of the giroh and since then, the wives often gave him leftovers: buttermilk, scraps of vegetables and meat. However, all he could predict now was a 'stupendous' recovery of a child from cough and cold or the death of a cat.

One afternoon, when the hot Chambal sun had sapped all their energy and goodwill, Lala and others sat around Dado, as they often did, trying to make his violent temper flare up. A full moon in the sky lit the scene, shimmering off the sikris and throwing dim shadows around the men.

'So what does your third eye tell you today, Dado?'

Dado was at first indignant, and haughtily claimed that the future could not be seen upon command.

Upon insistence, he grimly said, 'Mmm. Let me see.' He closed his eyes for a full minute, and he gasped, and screamed. With a hand on his heart, he panted, 'Do not go on a loot tonight, Lala. I foresee danger.'

'Says who? The man who foresaw the death of a chicken?' Lala retorted to resounding laughter from the other men.

'It is a full moon night. The angrez have a temporary tent right outside this jungle. You will get caught . . .'

'There are enough rocks to hide behind, Dado. Besides, has anyone ever caught me?' Lala winked and the other drunk men ferociously shook their head, cheering Lala.

Lala jumped up, saluted him, shook the old man's hand as he would the policeman's—an old joke, lost on the soothsayer all these years.

'Be careful, boy,' Dado said, turning into his sikri as Lala and others sauntered away, sullen and drunk, but adamant on proving the old Dado wrong. In the middle of the encampment, they conducted *bhaav*, a ritual Kanjar Bhatus particularly revered, before leaving for the loot. They gathered in solemn circles around a *bhopa* in a secret temple in Rawali, near Kota[16] as they conducted the bhaav, circulating a full bottle of liquor while chanting. The direction the bottle stopped in, they would head that way. Before big heists, they'd offer sacrifices of animals, dipping a thumb in the blood of the carcass and pressing it to their foreheads.

Those Kanjars who cannot go down to the temple perform the bhaav at home, with the encampment's bhopa in tow. If the bhaav or the spirit in the bhopa predicts a rotten hand, they cancel the plans, sit at home and wait for the fortunes to turn.

Lala and his aide had left that night for a nearby village with *dohatiyas* hidden along their backs; their faces, half-eclipsed by masks. Just when they were about to flee with the thick wads of cash, the moonlight startled them with an unnatural sheen, as if it were filling the room with ice. An officer appeared in the doorway in his night clothes and soon after, they were being ambushed by the British troops. The police chased them through the waters of Kalsindh; mid-river, the undertow was strong and the aide's leg slipped on a boulder underneath, while it rained in thick sheets. A gharial, lounging on the rocky bank, charged towards the aide, its teeth bared beneath its scaly snout.

Hoonkar, a toddler then, was at their giroh, watching his mother making her special halwa, when the news arrived. Thunder rolled and a hen outside rushed into the sikri to lay her eggs. His uncle tightened his lips as he came to deliver the news. Asan bai's hand was suspended in the air; the news was catastrophic enough to let the halwa burn.

Just before leaving for the loot, the Kanjars take an oath, or a promise, which to them is everything. The night before, Lala had taken out a silver bowl from one of the bundles in his sikri, brought the empty bowl to his lips and kissed it, closing his eyes, holding his breath as if tasting the tenacity of his ancestors. Later, his wife had poured in kaccha khatiya and some goat blood into the bowl. Sipping on it, Lala had given an oath or a pledge of loyalty to the gang and acceptance of the consequences if a breach of trust was made. And most important was keeping in mind the gang's safety and security.

Lala, being Lala, had made it his business to save his aide; he split open the gharial's mouth and chucked pebbles from the bank down its throat. The gharial writhed in pain, swinging its tail this way and that while Lala carried his gang member safely to the bank. The police, who managed to catch up with them, were witness to Lala's magnificent resilience. Purportedly, to bring him down, they shot an entire gun of bullets into Lala's wide chest as he swam to the bank while the aide escaped into the ravines. Minutes later, Lala's bloodied, mangled body was lifted by police—still struggling and fighting, despite the spreading bullet poison—and thrown into a trench. He struggled to breathe, weighed down by his own weight, as the soil piled above him, mixing with the salty tears from the heavens. They dug his body into the earth while he struggled to break free. Lala's bones were discovered by his brothers, months later, when a shepherd showed them the burial site about five kilometres from Harnavadha.

The morning after Lala's death, the sky was like a calm ocean. While the rest of the gang went about their work ruefully, Hoonkar's mother, Asan bai, lay in the tent, broken glass bangles piled beside her along with a change of clothes, a pale brown that women from the giroh thought was more suitable for her widowed state. Hoonkar, who was just five years old then, fiddled with the broken bangles, perhaps to fill the silence. Asan bai slapped Hoonkar, and then hugged him to her chest, sobbing as she told him that he would not go for loots with his uncles any more, and she would not do any cooking; henceforth, they would spend their days and nights inside the tent.

Little Hoonkar refused. He joined the other thin children who ran around with their naked bottoms in the grove. Many of the children collected unusable pieces of loot—boxes, wires, strings and bags—and traded them with each other. They climbed trees, held pretend axes made of bark; from high up on the branches, they threw inedible fruits down, making bomb-like sounds with their mouth. Diligently, they chased lizards around the bushes, catching them by their tails and roasting them over the fire.

At first, his mother was annoyed by his innocence while she sat on the floor in the sikri, crying, sweating and imagining her husband struggling for breath as he was buried. She was afraid to sit on the mattress because she might doze off and be unprepared when the police found their giroh and burnt it.

But deep down, it was not Lala she was worried about. They hardly talked, and when they did, he talked and she, with a veil covering her face, listened. Even on days he did not return home, she had said nothing to him. Asan bai refused to worry about him. She had worried about other things: how her ten-year-old daughter was still fitting into a five-year-old's clothes; how her grain stock was quickly depleting; what if her son was not a natural at robbery. With the help of the only lantern in the tent, she had opened a trunk of wheat grains; plunging her hand into its yellow, sand-like depths, she'd pulled out two necklaces, a bag of gold coins and a silver bowl. All Lala did was collect wooden figurines, green necklaces and perfume bottles that seemed of no value. How would she marry her daughters with these?

Even in the underworld, nepotism has its doles. Among the dacoits, Asan bai discovered over time, Lala's name was an asset even after his death. The bond between Kanjars was based on misery and secrets, and the encampment, according to the ancient verbal code, would look after his family. There were fixed amounts of shares to be paid from future robberies if a member died or was in jail due to an act of robbery, or had lost a limb during one, or even if he became impotent due to an injury to the testicles.

The closest relationships developed between people who endured fear, threats and violence together; in this case, his uncles and other relatives who lived in their giroh. The men in her giroh thought Hoonkar was brilliant because he was Lala's son. His uncle, or his father's brother, took it upon himself to make him as good as Lala was.

When he saw the police passing their giroh, little Hoonkar was taught to shriek like a peacock. On hearing a wayward traveller approaching their camp, he whistled, soft and low, like a *shama* bird.

'A Kanjar Bhatu never fears dark, or small, suffocated places,' his uncle told him; dragging him away from other children who sat under a tree and sucked oranges. With his fingers, the uncle built an imaginary hole, big enough for a rabbit to scrape its skin as it passed. 'Like a baby in the womb, you should sit inside holes until the police leaves.' After every lesson, he was given three smacks on the head, lest he forgot.

In his first lesson, his uncle demonstrated four ways to hide a stolen ring or a small knife in the extended orifices of the body: cheek, upper lips and throat. 'The last hole is not in the mouth, but the other end,' his uncle revealed, with a self-satisfied smile.

'The other end?' Hoonkar asked.

'Is something wrong with your ears? Your *gand*, the hole in your ass.'

'This, however,' His uncle boxed his ears before adding, 'comes with clear rules. Gold may not be kept "there". Gold is our watering well; it should not be debased by wearing it below the waist.'

During the day, they would go on excursions with his gang to the melas in the villages. On seeing a well-dressed man, one of his uncles would make a great show of beating him up. Hoonkar would then scream and yell, and rush for protection to the large-hearted, and large-pocketed, well-dressed man. Vicious with anger, the uncle would try to snatch the boy away. At last, when the sympathizer would convince the uncle to let the young boy go, he would find that his purse had disappeared too. Coconuts, shoes, soap, snacks—they pilfered whatever they came across.

They looted on days around the new moon, using darkness as a shield. On other days, they planned their travels, sold the loots through middlemen and worked on their skills. Hoonkar would practise digging holes with a *dohatiya*, a long iron rod with sharp end that could crack open locks too. 'Around Chambal,' his uncle taught him, 'where the doorsills are paved, you should simply dig deeper until you reach the sand; nobody layers more than two rows of bricks under the door.' Besides, he was also taught to rear lizards, and through their movement, determine the gaps in doors and walls. And dogs. What would they do without dogs? Hoonkar learnt to tame wild dogs which travelled with him, warning him of strangers and dangers.

'Poison a man with datura[17] seeds after he has been out all day in the hot month of Asadh,[18] the police will assume it's a heat stroke. When using arsenic, remember to burn the dhoti in which you pound it. Heal your bones by taking a dip in a bath of cow dung. Always ask your wife to stock herbs and roots like *gudbel, khadadar, dholi musli, kali musli, ashwagandha, shilajit* and *haldi*—steal them from the village *vaid*'s home; they heal the most vicious bites of dogs and gun injuries.'

'Don't rob when you can steal, and if necessary, kill,' his uncles would repeat before every loot. 'We are, after all, Rajputs.' And the cardinal Rajput virtue is heroism, not pity or modesty. The greatest fear for Kanjar Bhatus is not death, but divulgence of the *gupt pachan*, or the secrets of their community. It was there, that festering fear, that underlay everything they thought and did. *Chaurasi Buddhiyan*, or the eighty-four wisdoms, was their essential verbal handbook, full of rules, modi operandi, ancestral practices and regulations of matters. There were other rules to follow to ensure a successful dacoity: abstaining from sexual intercourse before a loot, taking baths and praying to the Din Devata; no molestation, rape or even eyeing another woman before or during the loot; no chopping off the feet of people whom they need to injure during the loot. And most importantly, never break down or reveal the gang's whereabouts and other details, no matter what the hardship in jail.

Once, Hoonkar's cousin had revealed the details of their whereabouts in jungle when in remand. When he was released, the bus that brought him back from the prison toppled into a canal. His body was found along the bank, a leg chewed up by a gharial.

\* \* \*

After Independence,[19] the Indian government, under the guidance of Nehru and Ambedkar, replaced the Criminal Tribes Act with the Habitual Offenders Act, 1952. But far from improving their lives, the new Act only re-stigmatized the marginalized tribes.

Today, several variants of these 'ex-criminal' and ex-nomadic tribes, such as the Pardhis, Kanjars, Ramoshis and Vanjaris, continue to be seen as a threat to rooted, settled villages. They may have moved out of the jungles, but they still live in separate encampments outside the villages, hidden behind long cobs of corn fields or tall trees or a rough ravine. Flies perch atop their kurtas as they make kaccha khatiya, or what they call Kanjar whiskey, in the dark shadows of moonless nights. Children cry often, as if they too realize that their houses are too close to each other's.

In Hoonkar's hut, his belongings are never on the shelf: scissors, pen, clothes and ID cards are always together in bundles or boxes. They may not be nomads any more, but they can't break this habit of keeping things close in case they need to run. Pandits sprinkle water from the Ganga when they pass by; other men and women protest

when their encampment is too close to the village, often
destroying the Kanjars's homes or burning them down;
even the poorest Chamars refuse to take work from them.
They are subjected to headcounts on account of their
being considered habitual offenders by the state, or their
settlements are made close to the police station. Often,
the members of such tribes become easy replacements for
criminals whom the police fail to apprehend. It's easy then
for them to be trapped in the soul-killing, gravitational
pull of the judicial system; survival then becomes a daily
hustle and their relationships with neighbours and society
are coarsened and befouled by that hustle.

* * *

In the late 1980s, Hoonkar had forgotten to line his eyes
with the auspicious *surma* or kohl before a dacoity. It was a
mistake, he realized, as they reached the loot site.

'Let's return,' he said and started to drive back,
talking to the others sitting with him in a newly acquired
mini-truck.

'But we are halfway to the merchant's house,' the others
protested.

They managed a fairly big heist that night: thousands
of rupees in cash, jewellery worth a woman's dowry and
a television. Hoonkar felt sated, knowing the loot hiding
beneath the cartons of oranges would keep his giroh secure
for years. The younger boys drank from the bottles as the
truck flew over the kaccha road, the trees disappearing
faster than they appeared. Hoonkar smoked in the front

seat of the truck, saving his appetite for the laal maas his wife had promised him. Just then, the front lights of the truck shone down on a man standing at distance, in the middle of the road, bringing the truck to a screeching halt.

With a polio-ridden leg, the man dragged himself to the truck and over the wind, he shouted, 'I have been walking for hours, *kaka*. Give me a ride; I work in the next village.'

Work at two in the morning, Hoonkar thought. He stared at the man's face; there was nothing that suggested malice.

'Which village do you belong to?' he asked the man.

'Jhalawar. I wouldn't ask if it was not urgent.'

Jhalawar, Hoonkar recalled. It was where he had met Lali, the beautiful Lali. He had gone back a few years ago with a necklace for Lali, but the baraadari had shut down; its women had left for Agra and Delhi, the locals said. In what was once a splendorous courtyard, clothes dried on a line and a few naked children played hide-and-seek beneath them. He had sat outside, eating jalebis in milk, imagining the tabla that once resounded in these ruins.

Hoonkar stared at the limp, and then shifted away from the window seat to accommodate him.

Minutes later, he a felt the cold jab of a gun in his side.

Hoonkar and his gang members that night faced jail for a month, but that wasn't what troubled him. He made it easy for the police to get hold of their gang and someone who betrays and dishonours the gupt pachan must be punished, he told himself. In custody, he and two other of his aides were defiant: They refused to talk to prosecutors, revealed nothing to the cops after days of being beaten up and dismissed pain and death as inevitabilities.

During the first week in jail, he could not sit on one part of his injured back, and so he lay on his side. He did not need the echo of pain to remind him of a robbery at that merchant's house, the little boy whom they had killed, the stark loathing in the mother's eyes before they hit her on the head. In the few hours that he slept, he had a recurring dream where he saw the merchant's house, smelt the chicken they ate from the kitchen, and heard the screams of the mother:

'No, leave him. Not him, that's my son . . .', but it was not her son that he imagined killing, but his own son.

When he woke up sweating, a prisoner sharing his cell offered him a cigarette.

'Fuck you!' Hoonkar muttered, walking away. He had urinated in his sleep.

The next time, he went to jail for a crime he did not commit. Several fields in a neighbouring village owned by a member of a certain Gujjar tribe had been looted of their crop overnight, and Hoonkar was taken in as a suspect. 'We do not steal from Gujjars, sir,' Hoonkar pleaded before the superintendent. 'How can we? Historically, our ancestors did *vanshavali varnan*, or maintaining of genealogy records, for them; our women sell goods and dance for them, for food and money. There is much respect between our communities. It must have been the thakur who wants to take revenge on me for refusing his work.' That earned him several more beatings and another week in prison.

When he was released, he went straight to the house of the thakur, a gregarious, plump man with the easy-going warmth of one used to importance. He sat in the chair with the highest back, and several gold chains clung to the folds in his neck. Here, the thakurs were still the apex of the human system, above various local worthies who sat beside him—a commissioner of police, a something in the chief minister's office. Hoonkar stood before them, his apology twisting him with remorse. His legs wobbled in despair, reacting to invisible spankings as he pleaded to the thakur for his protection. It was understood between the thakur, his aides and Hoonkar from that point on that he was his patron—and the thakur would employ him, if he so pleased, as a watchman, a thief or 'to push down others if they held their head too high'. The police officer, meanwhile, unofficially sanctioned this settlement, turning a blind eye to their activities or writing off the cases for a small part in the loot.[20]

* * *

Decades later, in 2001, under pressure from politicians, the police accepted the surrender of Hoonkar and his gang, nullifying all old cases registered against him.

The new chief minister of the state was from this area and could not afford the Kanjars bringing ill repute to her constituency. The girohs were given small patches of land to cultivate around the villages, but the Kalsindh, by then, hardly had any water. With no skills apart from deceit, the drug that crime was, and the complexity, substance and enthusiasm that it provided, withdrawn from their lives, Hoonkar could do little but make the illicit kaccha khatiya in the nights and sell it to unlicensed liquor shops. His sons started working as contract labourers in other farms while he became a night watchman in the fields and homes of well-heeled villagers, guarding against wild animals, trespassers and, much to his chagrin, robbers. Hoonkar could never get too far from the settlement, since he and others at the giroh had to give attendance to the police.

When the drought came that year, Hoonkar had to line up before a charitable nobleman's house, who donated food every morning to the 'desperately poor' on the insistence of a pandit, so that further good luck and fortune may come to him.

The first time he went to an affluent man's house, a large crowd had gathered outside the gates of the haveli much before it opened. Hoonkar stood awkwardly in the queue of ordinary villagers, not knowing what was more polite: keeping his hands by his side, behind his back or on his waist. He felt guilty, as if he was doing something improper: expecting to get food for the day without snatching or stealing it.

When the gates opened, he swayed as the crowds broke out of the queue and jostled ahead of him, as if shunting him out in one premeditated move since he was not one of them.

# 3

# THE KURUMBAS OF
# THE NILGIRIS

*A Kurumba rebel comes of age*

Coonoor, Tamil Nadu

Lying on the mattress, Mani follows the movement of his father's breathing. Moments ago, he had watched his father's sweaty hips thrust up and down while his stepmother, Bindu, lay still beneath him, muffling her pain. His father stayed silent, though maybe his lips kept moving—he was always moving his lips as though he were talking to someone invisible. A mongrel laid beside Mani's feet, its ears pricked for the sound. Each time his stepmother moaned, the dog yelped.

Like most other children in Hulikkal, a small village in the Nilgiris, Mani lives in one-room mud hut, where pots and pans are pushed aside every night to make room for mats, where they can hear their parents make love, or whatever else it is, through the mosquito net that hangs between them. He shifts on the floor; his upper back hurts from being slammed against walls by his angry father when he had come back jobless from the Badaga village. 'I can't pay for the giant morsels you eat any more,' he had shouted as he thrashed Mani. Mani wonders what it must be like growing up in the big Badaga houses he saw today, where children sleep in different rooms, thick brick and cement walls separating them from their parents.

He had not seen anything quite like the homes that appeared in the Badaga village: concrete square structures with windows painted smooth in purple, green and blue, with large vegetable patches or a stretch of tea estate sloping down in front. Each home had a little chimney with smoke swirling from it like the incense sticks his father used for the pujas. The trees and bushes were all trimmed; from the top of the hills, he could see fields of tea, with men and women moving through them, carrying their baskets on their backs, their feet stained red from the soil. When it rains in the Nilgiris, this red earth trickles like blood under its green skin.

Earlier in the day, Mani and his uncle had walked uphill after getting off the bus; the long walk had made his legs hurt, but that did not bother him. He was willing to cross many more such hills. In the absence of trees, that part of the Nilgiris was full of gusty wind that stung his eyes till tears stained his cheeks. When his uncle spoke, the winds carried his voice louder than he meant it to be, 'I told them you already know sowing'; he'd brought him here for a daily wage job at a tea garden. Mani nodded, although he'd hardly worked in fields: They had only a small plot where they grew vegetables and some millet. On other days, they ate what they collected—roots of yam, herbs and honey—from the forest where they lived or rice given to them by the government. This village, meanwhile, only housed the Badagas,[1] an educated, prosperous tribe that had migrated to the Nilgiris in the early twelfth century. The estate owner his uncle was taking him to had political aspirations and everything he did was to be transactional, driven by the desire to secure votes. Among his pet constituencies were the hamlets of the Kurumbas, also some of the poorest people in Nilgiris, and the area beyond.

'Call him *appa*,' his uncle insisted, in the Alu Kurumba language, a mix of Tamil and Kannada.

'Remember, you're a Kurumba. Do not stare at their family members.' Mani nodded, though his uncle had already told him this many times, just as he had told him to pat his hair down and not to say inane things: They are all educated, so don't talk any jungle hocus-pocus.

Mani wished people did not speak to him as if he were a jungle idiot; that said, he couldn't help but gape at the women who were walking their children to school. How smooth their skin was, their hair shining with oil, decorated with jasmine and plaited neatly with ribbons; their eyes, unlike the yellowed eyes of Kurumbas, were as white as their teeth.

Minutes later, Mani waited outside the Badaga man's house, while a few boys chatted on their way back from school, clapping each other's backs, laughing as they walked past him. Only a few from his hamlet went to school, but he could read what was written on their bag— 'Government'. He recognized the word from its shape—it was on every pamphlet and poster handed to them.

One of the boys said something that made the others shout with laughter. Mani bunched the hole in his shirt with his fist while admiring their uniforms. They then slowed their steps to look back at their friends coming behind them, signalling them to join. That was what he wanted to do when he got older—saunter with friends through these neat little hills, talk and laugh.

When Mani looked at them again, one of the them seemed to be pointing at him, at his hair matted like a mop on his head, teeming with vermin. After some whispering, one of the boys, pretending timidity, wrung his hands beseechingly before Mani, 'Spare me, oh Kurumba! Spare me from your sorcery,' and ran up the lane with the others, received by them with a hoot of laughter and much back-slapping. Mani had squeezed his eyes shut against the fierce brightness in which the boy's oiled head laughed and moved among the waves of sudden bright sunlight.

When he recovered his vision, Mani ran behind them, but only mustered enough courage to spit in their compound. Before the Badaga estate owner could see them, his uncle tugged at his wrist and hurried him back to the bus stop. The sun was sinking behind the mountains without any play of colours or movement, save for their flustered stomp downhill.

It was only in these last few years that his forest tribe, the Kurumbas, had started working in the fields of Badagas during the day. Until a few years ago, whenever the forest tribals came in view of a Badaga, word flashed through their village, and women and children ran for the safety of home, hiding inside till the Kurumbas had gone. If Mani knew a spell or two, he would have twisted those boys' knickers till they fell screaming from groin pain, and practise the sorcery that they claimed his people knew.

The Kurumbas, they said, had medicines that could put all the inhabitants of a Badaga village to sleep before slinking back into the woods. Their ace sorcerer, an *odikara*, could make openings in the fence, and the Badaga's livestock, under his spell, would follow him through it without so much as a cluck or a bleat. They could, apparently, turn into bears and kill people, just as they knew how to counter the other spells, to remove or prevent misfortune. Many decades ago, when the Badaga grandfathers were little boys still hanging from their mothers' waists, one of their elders returned from a Kurumba settlement situated outside the jungles, where he went to scout a plot for tea planting. He came back breathless, just about stuttering that their end was near and that a monster was around. Now, a Badaga knew that if a Kurumba sorcerer was casting spells, he could be appeased with rice, oil, salt and clothes. But what was this big brown animal he was screaming about, its eyes glowing red?

As the story goes, the goats, hens and cows were restless; they knew for certain that the elderly man had seen an irate Kurumba-turned-monster. All night, they howled in their sheds and tapped the ground, and the villagers slept fitfully, imagining figures and shapes in the hilly darkness.

The Badaga elders today still fear the sorcerer Kurumbas, often banding against them; their school-going children, though, have less faith in the Kurumbas's magical abilities. 'Isn't your father, what is his name . . . Moopan?

The limping old man who pretends to be a doctor?' a boy had teased Mani at the bus stop.

The Kurumba magic was wearing off, and a pervasive sense of futility remained. There it was, a distant murmur telling Mani that this fat Badaga life was not his birthright; there was always the possibility of running into people who spoke in hushed whispers around him; always a chance that however clean a shirt he wore, a passer-by may assume from his yellow eyes and uncouth hair that he was not a farm owner but the son of Moopan, the limping old sorcerer. His uncle had fallen asleep on the bus ride back home; Mani's eyes burnt as he looked out at the rolling tea estates of the Badagas.

The Kurumbas are the descendants of the Pallava dynasty, once powerful throughout southern India. In about the seventh or the eighth century, the final overthrow of their sovereignty was affected by the ferocious Chōla king Adondai,[2] causing the pastoral occupants, the Kurumbas, to scatter far and wide. Many fled to the hills in and around the Nilgiris, surviving on the bare minimum. However, separated from each other, and scattered among the Dravidian clans with whom they have dwelt, the Kurumbas are still regarded as some of the oldest inhabitants of the Indian subcontinent, and perhaps, 'contest with their Dravidian kinsmen, in the priority of occupation of the Indian soil.'[3] Soon, plainsmen like the Badagas migrated into the hills from the fallen Vijayanagar empire, stagnating the growth of local, native tribes like the Todas and the Kurumbas.

An agriculturist tribe, the affluent Badagas made immense progress in the 1850s when the British started turning large tracts of natural forests into coffee, tea, pine and eucalyptus plantations. The Kurumbas, however, still dwelt in the jungles. Recently after Independence, the government's restrictions meant to protect native forests and wildlife have forced them to move to the edges of the forest, where they earn their bread from selling forest produce and working as daily wage labourers.

Behind closed lids, faking sleep on the mattress, Mani can hear the night sounds of summer get louder as the moans from the bed subside: the chk chk of crickets, the untimely cackle of a laughing thrush or the swoosh of a night-time owl. Sometimes, a rectangle of light appears on their *dharbha* or thatched grass ceiling through the solitary window, the rectangles of lanterns that the Kurumba night watchmen take to the fields of Badagas to perform *panti-odi* or garden sorcery, that is, purveying magical protection to their fields to drive away elephants and pigs. When a Kurumba sees a wayward elephant in the field, he immediately starts muttering protective chants under his breath and then runs towards it with a burning torch made of bamboo; once he gets the torch close to its trunk, the elephant never fails to take flight. Should they attempt to run away, the elephant will chase them and put them to their death. But whether it is darkness, spirits or wild animals, no Kurumba fears anything. Mani, meanwhile, fears his father's loathsome life.

The story is told in Hulikkal of how his father, Moopan, was the only Kurumba ever in the village to be injured by an animal, and not an elephant or a gaur, but a mere dog. Inebriated, he was lying under a tree when a wild dog approached him in the hope of a meal. His father woke to a wet sandpaper lick from the dog and let out a scream before trying to scramble away. A villager ran to the spot and killed the dog with his axe, but not before the dog had torn into his leg. After that day, every time Moopan walks through the hamlet, the children sing the limerick, 'There goes a wimp, with a limp.'

When his father's snores get louder, Mani quietly slips out of the hut, barefoot. It is almost dawn; he walks out to the edge of the hill where he can see the Nilgiris, the blue mountains. They are the bluest when he lies down on his side and looks through the green that grows by his cheek. He watches a yellow butterfly perch on a blade of grass that bends under its weight. His birth mother would often bring him here; she wove cane baskets while he painted on rocks with a piece of cloth and paints made from soil and the barks of trees.[4] His hands were like a magician's, making intricate figurines dance around a tree full of bee hives; or another of sticks of men in white lungis playing drums hanging from their necks.

His mother's love for him was odd. She'd often stare at him and smile, sadly.

'Will you go to school, Mani? she asked him a year ago.

'What do they do in school?

'You learn about rivers, forests and mountains.'

'But that I already know. Our mountain turns purple with *kurinji*[5] flowers once in twelve years. If you break a bone, you must find a discarded deer antler in the forest and have it with pepper. The river that . . .'

'That is all good. But when you go to school, you can get a job. With a job, you can buy a bicycle and eat chicken.'

'OK, *aji*. I will go to school and learn a job.'

The day his uncle, his mother's brother, had picked him up after his first day at school in a nearby town, Mani walked out sulking. He decided he wouldn't go to school again.

'She made me sit in the back of the classroom, unlike the Badaga boys,' he complained to his uncle about the teacher. 'In the interval, I asked her when I would be taught a "job"; she slapped me.'

'Your mother is sick,' his uncle said, as if he had not heard anything else. 'She may die.' Mani was quiet for the rest of their long walk back to their hamlet.

She may die? But she only had stomach aches. Don't Kurumbas die only when they get old or their body is full of blisters? For everything else, there were spells and forest medicines. As he walked back from school that day, Mani played a secret game with his fingers that children in Hulikkal played. If he sang a song and it ended on an odd finger, his mother would live. So he sang a song and it ended on his odd finger. Pleased, he tried again; this time it ended on an even finger. He tried many times and made sure he said one or two words a little slow so that it ended on the odd fingers.

The next day, they buried his mother. His father remarried a girl half his age within a month of his mother's death. While they exchanged betel leaves and areca nuts as part of the marriage rituals, Mani sat here, in his favourite spot in the hills.

It is dawn by the time he walks back downhill to his village, a collection of seven or eight huts with no approach road. Bindu, his stepmother, waits for him outside the hut. She is small, thin and like all the Kurumba women in their hamlet, her sari is tied in a knot over her bosom.

'Where were you? Your food is ready': Her silky voice hypnotizes Mani; a strange feeling shoots up his stomach when her hand strokes his head. He has seen dogs doze off when someone barely strokes their heads like this. He pictured himself thrusting her, like his father did last night. What if his father knew what he was thinking? As the stepmother purrs him on to eat more, Moopan sits outside under a broken solar light, drunk before the sun has set: a short, dark-skinned man with the same mop of head over his head as his son; a wide nose and deep yellow eyes like that of every Kurumba in Hulikkal. Finishing his last swig of liquor, he is wiping his lips with the back of his hand, rotating his neck as if trying to recalibrate himself.

In the time Moopan is not drinking, he administers medicines to other tribes whose families, or *seemey*[6], he did pujas for. Besides possessing extraordinary spiritual powers, Kurumbas also act as healers by curing ailments; they are especially good at curing piles, joint pain and even diabetes. Flowers, roots, leaves, dry bark, tender twigs,

climbing tendrils, twining shrubs and seeds which they dare not reveal the names of, for the fear of reducing the Kurumba power and their knowledge: These plant materials are mixed with jaggery, breast milk, small onion, pepper, turmeric and oils. Moopan, though, has only half the stock of these medicines, which are mostly foraged from the forest; most of his time goes in to procuring his liquor from vendors.

'My head swims all day. It feels like I'm submerged in water,' complains his patient, who lives in a village downhill.

Just when Mani thinks he is going to pass out, Moopan half-opens his eyes and pours some coconut oil and sesame oil on his fingers, slopping most of it on the mat below.

'I see black spots everywhere. It is like the worms of the water have made way to my brains through my . . .'

Moopan raises his hand, indicating that he has already figured out his ailment, and shuts his eyes again, muttering a chant under his breath.

Now, a Kurumba healer would have studied his eyes, his rolling tongue, the corners of his fingers or the tightness of the head. But his father is too drunk to remember this; just as he forgets to first offer the medicine to the round black stone, called Hiriadeva, before administering it to the patient.

*'Peru mande-bettu peru male po*
*clru mande-bettu ci'ru male po*
*atti-pu: karagunatte . . . kar . . .'*

(Big headache, go away to the big mountain
Little headache, go away to the little mountain
As the blossoms of the fig trees have withered away, thus
wither away)

In the middle of the chanting, Moopan rotates his neck
fiercely. The spirit of his ancestors, purportedly, has
entered his body by now: the one that will heal and
cure his patients. Then in the dark void, he screams in a
terrible voice, 'I see a pair of legs dangling from a mango
tree behind your house and feel the contempt of this man
radiating in . . .'

'But I have no mango tree behind . . .'

'Why, this evil spirit,' he screams louder, pausing for a
burp, 'has chosen to finish generations of your family and
kill them.'

'Oh, Lord Siva! What must I do? I'm a poor man.'

'*Ame curundatte curundu* (as a tortoise has retreated
into its shell, thus retreat),' he starts chanting again, but
lies back against the wall, closing his eyes.

'Rice . . . donate . . .' Moopan slurs, 'clothes and oil and
sacrifice a hen. And rub . . . oil . . .'

'Where? On my head?'

Before Moopan can answer that, he falls flat on his face.

'*Aiyo aiyo* . . .' the patient yelps, running out of the
house. The village headman shouts behind him, 'Poor
Moopan is tired from hosting spirits.'

There is nothing more to do here, Mani sighs. If the
patient recovers, he will have to send across gifts as pots,

pans, hens and a dhoti, but should the man die or his health worsen, Moopan would be offered verbal sympathy for having had to tackle so potent an adversary, and the patient would end up at the government hospital in Ooty. Not only him, generations in his family have been traditionally coming to Moopan's family for medicines and cures. Till a few years ago, Moopan used to make a fair living curing their illnesses and providing them with incense, bamboo poles, resin and other religious products for pujas that he collected from the forest. They say he could discreetly source particular varieties of plants and leaves for performing black magic or for undoing it, but it is impossible to ascertain the names of those plants or herbs from the Alu Kurumba medicine men and magicians because they strongly believe that if the names of such plant species are revealed to others, the medicines lose their potency and that act also invites supernatural punishment.

Each Kurumba had the religious duty, shorn of financial motives, of taking care of a certain number of families living in a Badaga hamlet. The pastoral Todas provided the ghee and milk; the Kota craftsmen and musicians furnished others with pots and music at festivals, while the agriculturalist Badagas would provide the grains. They stood in the same exchange relationship with the forest-dwelling Kurumba, who could only provide meagre material compensation like the honey gathered from the forest, cane goods and, occasionally, herbs and fruits. But the Kurumba gave, instead, supernatural protection, since the Kurumba was the dreaded sorcerer; so feared that every

Badaga and Kota family had their own Kurumba protector against their own magic.[7]

So Moopan conducted little pujas for timely and plentiful rains, or to protect the fields from animals. He sowed the first handful of grains for the Badagas every season. On the day of sowing, Moopan would set up a stone in the field, decorate it with wild flowers, offer incense, and then sacrifice a goat. At the harvest, he received some of the grains, tea or other produce, trading his services based largely on the extraordinary dread of his supposed magical powers. They could, as their elders said, attract wild animals to their fields at will or turn their hills into powder by scattering herbs on them. Some of the Badaga families, however, had stopped sending goods to Moopan: 'That drunk weasel! He can hardly stand on his legs, forget poisoning us with his sorcery.'

Although Kurumbas can be found all over Kerala, Karnataka and Tamil Nadu, the Nilgiris were inhabited mostly by a group known as the Alu Kurumba[8] tribe. They lived as hunter-gatherers and used the slash-and-burn method for small millet cultivation until recently. Back in 1901, when Thurston,[9] a British Indologist, first conducted a study on the Kurumba tribe in the Nilgiris, the term 'Alu Kurumba' was absent; it seems to have been a recent development, probably a few decades old. Alu in Kannada means milk, implying good and harmless, like the milk. It is quite possible that in order to clear out or impair the negative opinion of them by the local people, developed due to their traditional practice of sorcery and witchcraft, the Kurumbas (of this part of the Nilgiris) themselves added the prefix of Alu to their general identity of Kurumba, for an improved status and wider acceptability. But to this day, there is minimal visiting back and forth, and no easy exchange of ideas or skills between the various tribes of this part of the Western Ghats. The Kurumba maintain their isolation in this sense as firmly as do the Todas. If it is true that the groups are mutually dependent, it is equally true that each fiercely insists upon its uniqueness.[10]

On most evenings, Mani ends up at Siva's place in the next hamlet, where boys gather in the evening. Siva refuses to work as a labourer 'in fields of pudgy-bottomed Badagas'; he sits outside his *kotte*, bare-chested, amid coiled bamboo ribbons, stripping and softening long strips of the wood. He never married or had children, and eked out a living for himself by making cane goods. Often, he disappears for days, returning with scratches and bruises; the explanations run counter to Siva's mode of being. Why does anyone need to know what he is thinking, when they can all see what he is doing? He has developed a passion for wandering and sometimes he roams so far that he has to spend nights in the forest; if you catch him in the mood, he will tell you about his forest adventures: a frail rope bridge from ancient times that he walked between two hills, and before his eyes, it fell into the valleys deep below; a waterfall that was climbed with his naked hands. No one knows whether he is telling the truth, because no one from their hamlets has walked as far and as wide as Siva has; even beyond the Nilgiris. Mani is fascinated with

Siva: He is mysteriously full of knowledge of things that are alien, and different—nuclear wars, plump red fruits called strawberries, charming women with gifts from the forest, Marx and Lenin. He secretly wants to learn these things, so he lurks in his shadows when he can before he has to go back home and the spell is broken, before the adult world, with its ordinary disappointments, presses in.

'Want to smoke?' Siva interrupts, as Mani tells him about his visit to the Badaga town. He has probably heard such stories, even been a victim, many times before.

Mani nods, holding the stub of beedi between his fingers.

'My neighbour takes a bath in that spring. She usually does it around now. She takes care of herself in there.'

'What do you mean?'

'See,' he says, exhaling, 'you're just a little kid, *mutthal*. When I was your age, I did all sorts of wrong things. But I did them so I don't have to do them now.'

Mani had touched himself for first time a few weeks ago, when the other siblings were fast asleep on the floor beside him; he thought of his stepmother—the roundness of her cheeks, her smooth throat and then her breasts. He imagined sleeping on the soft lushness of her chest as she stroked his hair. But he couldn't tell all this to Siva, could he?

'There is hardly anything that you know, my boy. Before you know anything, you have to know what you don't know.'

'I know.'

'You know? *Othaa*! Fuck you.'

He walks to the edge of the hill and takes a last puff before tossing the butt into the valley.

Digging out a small cloth bag from his lungi, he unwraps, with enchantment, some leaves that were crushed with tobacco, and rolls it into another smoke.

'See, I was much like you when I was a kid.' Siva sighs. 'And here I am now . . .' He shakes his head, offering the smoke to him. Mani takes a deep puff; his head and stomach are completely empty, so the smoke leaves a vacuum within him.

'You understand castes?[11] The tribes here are like castes, only they call them tribes. Clean, nice, lighter-skinned people are Badagas, like the Hindu Brahmins. Todas and Kotas lie somewhere in between and we are like the untouchables or the Kurumbas. They have taken our forests, and given us.' He throws a sweeping hand at his hamlet, 'this land. Land, they call it? What will we grow here when all the water is taken by that *thailam maram* (eucalyptus), tea and silver oak planted by the British?'

Mani does not understand caste, but he feels angry. He feels like sucking in more air, as though it is rapidly deflating from some outlet other than his nose. What are those leaves that he mixed with the tobacco? It makes him feel strangely light-headed.

'I'm going honey-gathering tomorrow morning. There is a spot I had marked a few weeks ago. Be ready tomorrow morning.'

Mani jumps up immediately, eager to finally join him on one of the honey-gathering trips. He was hoping that his initiation on an apiary trip with Siva would be a bit of ceremony, where the other boys would enviously look at him depart with a vine ladder. Old grandmothers[12] of the hamlet would sing songs in the village square about honey collection; interspersed would be songs on elopement with lovers, extramarital affairs, abnormal sex organs, jackfruits, cucumbers, etc. The men would have played *tamabati*, or the drum, to which the younger women would dance in circles, clapping their hands together below the waist. Honey-gathering season began every year with these festivities in the village, culminating with the village priest performing an ancestral puja, calling on the ancestors for good luck and then muttering some Sula Devaru[13] incantations. But with Siva, Mani understands that this was how he did things, with spontaneity so conclusive that the whole question of a planned celebration seems somehow beside the point.

He sleeps with Siva that night, hardly sleeps, really; all night the wind is making sounds, a low inhuman buzz through the trees, and riled up by the wind, animals are calling out, responding. In the morning, with a small bundle of government-distributed rice in a bag, the two set out on an uneven path through the hilly jungles. The forests here have a few tigers, panthers, many elephants and bears. There are wolves too, most of them mere bones, so famished that it seems like they will chew on their legs if they could get away with it; they dare not harm a Kurumba, though, whose bag of incantations the animals greatly fear.

Mani looks around the forests, recalling the last time he was here, perhaps four or five years ago, when he came to pick forest wood with his mother: The green was so wild and thick back then that he could hardly see the hills through it. The streams had clear water, more transparent than air; they are used to the mist enveloping the hills, but once, it used to be the white of thin sheets of cloud. Now it seems like smoke from the cooking pots. A short walk from anywhere in the jungle, he can see neat tea plantations sloping down the hills.

'Those bastards have made a tea farm beyond this patch of forest,' Siva sniffs. 'The shola trees,[14] which the bees love, are gone. They have machines now that throw pesticides and fertilizers for more produce. More produce, bah! What do they need more money for?'

The jungle even sounds different, Mani thinks; there are fewer calls of kites and the woodpigeons; the tahrs are almost gone. Instead of the mulch, dry leaves crunch under his bare feet. Kurumbas always walk barefoot, a sign of respect they accord to Mother Nature. The duo zigzag their way around the tiny kurinji flowers; they have bloomed after twelve years despite the encroaching farms. Their purple spread has a practical purpose, to enrapture the bees, but it is hard not to see the kurinji spread symbolically, as a defiant assertion of life in the face of death.

Siva and Mani walk all day through the forest and over the hills. In the night, they camp under large rocks with cave-like formations, where bears usually make their home.

Mani sits before the fire, staring at the spitted bird that Siva has charred on it.

'What is wrong? You want the bigger piece?'

Mani shakes his head, squeamish at the tuft of bloodied grey feathers that he sees near the fire, but he still tugs at the meat, hungrily tearing the bird to slivers. As his feet warm by the remnants of the fire, he listens to the jungle coming alive in the middle of the night.

Each spring, as the wind dies down and clusters of jacaranda flowers bloom on the trees, Kurumbas sense the spring in the air and start following the bees in the forest— big, small or *nirjare*, the fly-like bees—as they collect sap from the flower. The pollen sticks to them, dropping as they buzz back to the hive, creating a trail. Months ago, Siva had followed these trails with his keen eyes, which led him to the hives; he marked them with a bunch of leaves attached to a stick on the ground below the hive to let other Iurumba and Irula[15] honey gatherers know that this was to be his produce, a rule most of them followed except an errant, whom Siva can set right with a smack or two. After scrutinizing the stage of development the honey is in, he returns in the summer to pick the mature honey.[16]

'With the hive I have marked, there will be at least one more pair hive nearby,' Siva tells Mani as they move to the cliffs early next morning. A queen bee produces around one or two baby queen bees. Once the new queens are ready to take charge, many worker bees go with them. While crossing a small brook, Siva points to a small, almost unnoticeable cavity on one of the cliffs, with melon-sized hives. Somewhere along the way, they had opened a jackfruit and, while eating, they built the tools for the task from scratch: a wooden spear from a tall branch, a rope fashioned from a strong *biscoti* vine to be used for swinging against the face of the cliff, along with a ladder they had brought, made from cane and the *suryakodi* plant. And then the *panthai*, a bunch of dried leaves of *vazhaipul* that Siva will hang from his back.

Siva climbs the cliff from the other side, finding one improbable foothold after another, climbing what seems like a smooth rock. Where is he finding the holes, Mani wonders, and yet, there he is, already up the cliff, tying the rope to a tree, and then descending to a point where he is level with the hive. From here, Siva could be of any age, not the forty-year-old man he was. He is still so agile and effortless in his movements—was this climbing how he got the cuts and bruises? But those bruises were uglier, unnatural.

A few minutes pass by with no movement; he hangs near a mottled scrubland that gives way to a dense line of trees. Mani watches him attempt to insert a hand into the hive, but he quickly withdraws it.

'*Adu ena.* Is everything okay?' Mani shouts out to him.

'There is a snake inside the hive. So the bees are refusing to let me touch the comb.'

A frisson of expectation, as palpable as a cold shadow, passes over Mani as Siva hangs cross-legged below the hive. He pulls out a *bugiri*, a flute-like instrument, from his trousers, playing it to the bees and then singing prayers, so they would listen to his call for honey.

Within minutes, a keelback slithers out, as if heated up by the incessant chanting, disappearing into the trees. Siva puts away the bugiri, immediately smoking the hive and a dark cloud flies out, buzzing furiously, angry at getting drugged by the smoke; it debilitates their senses and the bees either escape into the bushes or fall on the ground. Siva manoeuvres himself mid-air; all that lies between him and a deadly fall are his skills and the poise of the mountain. He slices the comb off with the spear, and into a basket that is tied to the end of the rope.

Mani pulls the pot down and marvels at the golden comb in it. Three or four reticent bees continue to fight him, but fall into their own honey after the fateful sting. His genes, over centuries, have developed immunity to the sting. Siva, though bare-handed, has never been stung; he has a gentle method with the bees, playing his bugiri, calming them before splitting open the hives. He gently speaks to the hive, as Mani admires him, 'Some for the forest, some for me,' he says, treating the hives with almost familial care, pouring out the golden honey into the basket, with a dead bee or two. The filtered honey will be used in their own homes and the surplus sold in the village markets. Mani climbs down the rope next, taking three or four more hives despite the burning stings on his arms. Hours later, they munch on the honeycomb dripping with honey, making their chins and fingers sticky. When they leave, Mani notices that Siva has left some of the comb for the forest—for the bears, birds and insects. The drowsy bees, meanwhile, will wake in a couple of days and carry on with the cycles of nature.

'You were good today. That cliff was not easy to climb,' Siva tells him as they walk back with the baskets on their heads.

Mani beams; the scratches on his knees feel like badges of honour, the stings feel like an initiation rite, and he marvels at them quietly. He is sore after a long day on the cliffs, but the appropriate thing to do, he learns, is to say little and to keep company with Siva, who says little about his own pain; this is his turn from boyhood into manhood.

Suddenly, he feels a raindrop and then another. The clouds are not in sight yet, but he can sense the stillness in the air.

'Let's go to this Kurumba settlement in the forest,' Siva tells him. 'They will host us for the night.'

Mani is relieved that they are not going home yet.

An emerald light surrounds the hamlet, which is a couple of minutes into the jungle on the fringes of a tiger reserve; nine or ten huts make up the *mulla vadi*, a village in the forest. The birds and other animals around them have gone quiet; the world is still as it can be only when bad weather is coming. A few children who were playing with marbles scatter and run after Siva. Clearly, Siva was no new face here. Outside, in one of the huts sits an old man, his face disguised by a thick mop of curls. As they get closer, Mani's jaw drops.

It is Nagan, a honey collector in the village who had disappeared a few years ago. Now maybe in his fifties, he no longer has the virile brown moustache of his youth, but his face has compensated by acquiring a patina of menace. Many assumed he was killed by the Badaga farmers who claimed that he, with his knowledge of necromancy, had caused many of their cattle to die.[17] For the Badagas, there was no greyness in the concept of evil; it was black magic coming from a particular person, so if you wanted to get rid of the evil spell, you finished the man. The same thing applied to goodness. Nobody could try to be good; you either had it in you or you did not. When their village headman lodged a complaint about Nagan's disappearance with the police, they dismissed the case because no one had seen him leave the village or knew where he went. 'Anyway, he seemed a bit erratic,' a constable drawled.

Running away from the village, which insisted he apologize to the Badaga for no wrong that he committed, Nagan came to live here, deeper in the forest, with this settlement of Kurumbas. They had been living in the thickest jungle for generations but were moved farther out by the forest officials, tea estate owners and collectors every year. Gravity has now given Nagan's mouth a permanent frown. His eyes are partially obscured by thick, drooping brows, and they are rheumy, as if he were harbouring a terminal hill disease.

'Come, Siva, come. I was expecting you. Did you get my stuff?' he asks.

Siva nods, handing him a pouch of tobacco.

'Who have you brought along?'

'Moopan's son.'

'Ah, that Moopan,' Nagan taunted, smirking, and immediately sparking a fire in the pit of Mani's stomach. Nagan was once known by all as a valorous hero who spoke up for Kurumbas and he did not want to be identified as a weakling's son before him.

'What do you do?'

Mani contemplated telling him about the few hours he spent loitering in the small plot allotted by the government for growing millet, but he simply shook his head.

'Nothing? Nothing is good. Out of nothing comes something. You did not go to school?'

'No, they made me sit separately.'

'Oh, look at him. You are old enough to know they made you sit separately? Siva, is this even that wretched Moopan's son? *Korangus*, monkeys! That is what they are, my child. What do those oil-pampered Badagas know about the world?'

The sky darkens and an unseasonal downpour starts as they run into Nagan's one-room hut, covering their honey baskets with extra leaves. The men sit down to smoke the tobacco. Nagan mumbles something to a middle-aged woman sitting on her haunches; her curly bob of black-and-grey curls rests on her shoulder, tied with a weed. She too had abandoned her village and joined Nagan when she saw him castigating a union of tea workers to demand higher wages. They were not married, but she lived with him and did his housework: cooking, cleaning and tending to his vegetable garden. Sitting before a fire in the shed, she heats up a pan, frying the onions, garlic and chillies, before adding the boiled lentils; water is added, and the pot is closed with a lid. She stirs every few minutes while chopping a quick salad of wild greens, green chillies and tomatoes. She then slowly grills a lardy-looking hog stomach, marinated with spices on a tender stem.

'You cannot die of hunger here, my boy.' Nagan laughs, the smoke from his mouth blending with clouds from the hills that pass between them.

'Berries, herbs, honey and tubers grow everywhere like weeds. That is why our people never learnt to work; they've never had to harvest and store food to survive. We Kurumbas just want to live here, in the forests, in these ancestral homes. For decades, the forest officials have falsely arrested us Adivasis on the slightest pretext, confiscated our knives, which we need to hack through the jungles. Last week, they asked us to move out of here. Too close to the forest, they say, and took away our honey, meat and fruit.'

Nagan protests their eviction from the jungles every time they are pushed farther out. Last year, he burnt a forest official's home. Another time, he destroyed their forest-touring vehicle. Like many other men and women who are recruited for the mission, Siva joins him too, training people for their movement; in the dense nights, he teaches the men from these hamlets how to make smoke bombs, and how to use the *koyalu kati*, or a sickle, as defence. They write the slogans on the walls of rich men in blood, and set many of their wattle, sandalwood and eucalyptus on fire. Many times, they have injured police officers and men from the village.

Nagan strolls away and returns with a bottle of liquor and a bugiri; he plays the flute that he has carved himself.

'So are you a Naxal?' Mani whispers to Siva as he drinks straight from the bottle.

'No, mutthal. They all want power. Them and the political organizations and the NGOs. All we want is to live peacefully in the forests.'

So this was how he got the bruises and the cuts, Mani realizes. Over the years, his body has been injured in the course of his efforts to harm others. Once, while attacking a post office to stage a protest, the police threw a smoke bomb in their hiding spot. Before Siva's aides could stop him, he seized the smoke bomb and threw it into a large clearing, where the wind could blow up the flame. He did not get up from the bed for a month after that episode; Mani remembers sneaking him pieces of chicken and a herbal paste from home in his pockets.

Providing shade to Nagan's house is a giant jambolana tree with so many hives that one can spend more than half a day standing under the tree, counting the hives. In the night, Nagan would work on plans to foil the attempts of these officials and during the day, he would play his bugiri, chant prayers to the 'stone' under the tree. Soon, multiple hives would emerge. At least twice a year, the men from the settlement collect the honey[18] and other forest produce, such as soapnut, myrobolans and dye barks, exchanging them for essentials like salt and clothes in the market near Hulikkal. The rest of the time, they forage, eat and sleep in these forests.

While Nagan plays the bugiri, Mani quietly sits on the briars on a spot in the dirt not worn bare yet; the not-quite-ripe jamun is plain against the less-black sky, and the summer air thick with moisture. He tries not to think about this time of the day in the village, when he is either sitting in the corner of the hut hearing the overruling roar of an angry, frustrated father who threatens violence, or idly walking the streets between Kurumba hamlets and other villages. He drinks the odd-tasting white liquor till he comes into a cloudy, buzzy-headed drunk state. But what he feels is something more intense than liquor. Two days in these forests and he does not want to go back to his village life. He does not enjoy working in the fields; that is not his life's purpose.

Afternoon gives way to the evening and the rains fade away, leaving pools of water between the rocks. A young man in a white loincloth and with a potbelly, and the visage of the hamlet fool, pretends to fight the rains with a stick; he frolics in the puddles, jiggling his belly as the kids laugh at him. Nagan continues playing while the rest eat the grilled hog; later, although his bruises still burn and sting, Siva, Mani and the others dance with the fool.

Sometime around dawn, Mani forces his eyes open; heat is warming his face, as if he has edged too close to the embers while sleeping. His eyes open to a fierce fire edging close to the settlement. For a moment, he is mesmerized by how stunning the growing flames look, leaping to capture bush after bush, tree after tree.

And then a woman's voice comes, screaming in the distance: 'My child! Where is my child?'

Loud voices, and then many men, fill the hamlet square; the huts empty one after the other, and the families gather their children and spill outside, running for the edge of the pasture. They help the old grandfathers to their feet and lead them to another hill; from here, they can see the hamlet swimming with shadows: the huts and trees and smoke. When the rains came earlier today, red earth and stones with nothing to hold on to poured downhill, following the same channels that pull the fire up the hill. It seemed like the hillocks are breathing: breathing in the flame, breathing out the mud.

There is nothing larger at stake here than eight huts, and nobody owns anything precious except work tools that can easily be salvaged from the fire, and yet the blazing stillness has the flavour of wartime menace.

'How did a forest fire happen after the rains?' someone asks.

'I could smell kerosene. It is arson,' Siva mumbles.

Clothes and face blackened from the soot, Nagan's eyes reflect the orange flames in front of him. 'Must be those wretched tea manager's men.'

'My bees are dying too,' he whispers. He pulls a bugiri from his shorts and begins playing. While nursing his own twisted ankle, all scratched up, and clothes torn like floor rags, Mani hums the tune too. It is the refrain of '*aare turati lede*', the song sung by the grandmothers when the men go honey-hunting.

Nagan's eyes meet Mani's. And he understands that it is true. They both had dropped out of school. Nagan had left his home. One day, he knew he would have to leave his home too. This, he feels, is the beginning of his real life, of everything he has been waiting for. Wind whiffles his cowlicks as he stares at the fire devouring the hamlet. He will join the movement and fight for their rights; he does not know where he will stay—tomorrow, he will sort it out. For tonight, he could stay here. In the open jungles.

# 4

# THE MARIAS OF BASTAR

*A girl who grew up in a ghotul and often
cooks meals for the Naxal cadre*

Bastar, Chattisgarh

In Bastar, life seems to grow unshackled, wild and often wanton: seeds, chucked by insects and birds, don't wait for a drizzle. They grow into a mahua here, a *salphi* there; by spring, they lug the weight of juicy fruits and sticky sap. At dusk, boys camping in the groves with a picnic of spicy red-ant chutney[1] and chicken go from palm to palm. After a little ceremony, a kind of Maria cocktail hour, they collect and drink the frothing fluid from the leaf cups. In a perpetual state of semi-intoxication, they dance from village to village for the rest of the season.

Sowed in this wilderness is an essential restrain that they practise in their everyday lives.

Birsu and Sukaru have been married for a decade and a half, but they had a child only six years ago, after many herbal concoctions and prayers. Birsu wakes up in the middle of the night, wondering what woke her up. Her stomach hurts, from the weight of her daughter's foot. Birsu shoves it aside, trying to go back to sleep, but her husband's snores keep her awake. She tosses and turns restlessly for some time, listening to the nocturnal sounds of the forest: the owls, some cats and a hyena. She takes a deep breath to inhale the smell of the woods, which always seems far more attractive to her than the smell of humans.

Sukaru works a few villages away as a dutiful peon in a government office. These days, he returns home tired: the flat glassiness in his eyes, the slump to his shoulders worry her. Waking up again with a start, Birsu reproaches herself bitterly for sleeping too long; the gruel should have already been ready before he left for work. Running her hand over his side of the mattress, she feels the last of the creased warmth. She must make him the fresh mahua flower liquor that he asked for last night; the cow has been tied in case it eats the mahua flowers before Birsu wakes up. It is at night that the tree blossoms and at daybreak, each short-lived flower falls to the ground.

It's not yet dawn, but the shadows have already lengthened by the time Birsu is in the forest. It is the time of the year when even the most ordinary-looking sal tree turns yellow, when a simple *akash bel* is stitched with white flowers. In her cloth bag, Birsu drops a slice of sal bark for her mother-in-law's joint pain; *datun* or neem twigs to clean their teeth with for the week; and a handful of tart berries as she walks over the forest mulch. Theft becomes a duty here; only a fool would leave *Bauhinia vahli*,[2] which it is fat with next season's seeds; or the yams for their midday meal, and *chironji*, the seeds of which she will roast for the porridge tonight. When she comes to the pond, Birsu sticks a knife into the chilly shallow water to fish. But the fish is so little and the water so nice, she swims instead. This is better than the toilet the government had built them: the bathroom floor was always slimy with dirt, and the air thick with smell.[3]

Gudari, a hamlet near Orchha in Bastar, Chhattisgarh, approachable by a steep walk uphill, is where Birsu and her Maria tribe have lived for centuries, seldom travelling beyond the market towns around the hills. These villages, in the dense forests of the Abujmarh hills, have long been isolated from the outside world, inhabited largely by the Marias and other sub-Gond tribes like the Murias and the Halbas. They are accessible only via forest pathways that are steep treks uphill from the nearest motorable road.

The Marias have come a long way since the 1800s, when Maratha officials described them as 'naked savages, living on roots and sprigs, and hunting for strangers to sacrifice',[4] and then in 1938, according to Grigson's account:[5] '. . . the women go with breasts uncovered. Very old women occasionally hobble about inside their huts completely naked.' It was only in the post-Independence years, when the tribes had already been introduced to missionaries and the Indian government, that younger women like Birsu started wearing blouses with saris and speaking both Halbi[6] and Gondi.[7] And yet, they still inhabit two worlds simultaneously, with hardly any schools, no hospitals, a megalithic culture, where for each clan there is, or was, there is a holy circle beneath a sacred *saja* tree, which in reality is their God, known as Bura Deo. The Marias worships hills, streams, trees and, above all, the forest, which always infringes on their backyards, where they grow vegetables, medicinal herbs and a mandatory *tendu* bush for tobacco.

Birsu knows that old man Ghoru's story was improbable—he had said that work on a new mine was starting deeper into the forest beyond Gudari. She knows she should not be venturing so deep into the woods to reach the hill; Sukaru's admonitions resounded in her ears. Ignoring the voice in her head, she quickly dries her hair, lugs the firewood on her head and nips along the path deeper into the forest. A short walk ahead, she sees a man and a woman farther down the stretch: They are in olive green, dirty uniforms, with guns hanging from their shoulders. Her knees almost give away; she looks at a banyan tree by the side, but the roots are too thin to hide behind.

She starts to run, but hearing the man loading the cartridge of the gun, Birsu stops in her tracks.

'Lie down. Do you have any money on you?' the woman shouts in Gondi.

When Birsu shakes her head, the woman pulls the bag off her. The weasel-faced man, or maybe a boy, shorter than the woman, looks on with a scowl while the woman pulls her close, shoving a stick at her chest. She is a stiff, with a static face and burning eyes; her fire seems to come from a faraway, deep hole within her.

These are the people she has seen moving in the jungles, at the foothills of the Abujmarh hills behind her village. In the night, they move with torches, looking like fireflies. In the day, the green of their uniforms rustles against the green of the jungle. The CRPF forces and police have set up camps everywhere the roads reach, but roads hardly reach anywhere in Bastar. For miles and miles, there are thick jungles and amid its prowling cats, the Naxals have charted their own paths and their own rules.

Emptying the bag on the forest floor, the Naxal woman kicks aside Birsu's forest pickings with minimal effort, lifting only a package wrapped in sal leaves, sniffing it coldly. She has probably not eaten a decent meal for hours, maybe days.

'Is that with mutton?'

'Yes,' Birsu mutters. She becomes aware of a stream of water licking its way down the end of her hair and slicing over her right hip. It feels dangerous, like a cold knife across her skin.

'This is good shit!' the man blurts out, scooping up the curry with his dirty fingers, baring his tobacco-stained teeth.

'Ah, my mother used to make it like this,' the woman says, pausing to belch. 'May the *angapen* rest her shitty old soul!'

'How old are you?' she asks Birsu.

'Not sure. I have a child.' This somehow enrages the Naxal woman and she slaps Birsu, pushing her to the ground. Disgust in her eyes, she spits on the ground beside her. 'Then we cannot take you to fight for the Adivasi. Your youth is wasted in bearing children.'

As the splintering light that had spread before her eyes fades away, Birsu notices the woman walking back into the forest with a hurried limp; polio, maybe, or a gunshot wound.

When Birsu returns home, she finds Radha, her daughter, on the path outside their home.

'They ate Krishna *behen*,' she sobs, phlegm and tears puddling on her chin.

'I cannot understand you, Radha,' she rubs her temples after putting the firewood away.

'Those men in green clothes ate Krishna—that urchin girl at the *ghotul* whose parents died last year,' shrugged the grandmother, stirring a curry in a pot on an open fire outside. 'Last night, two men and a woman had come in from the jungles and took our hens. Krishna was heard screaming,' she says. A patrolling officer who came in from that side of the jungle said that those hungry Naxals roasted her on a pit. He says it is pointless looking for them; they must have already receded deep into the jungles.'

Birsu has a sudden urge to vomit; she wipes Radha's cheeks and nose with the end of her sari. Giving her some dried fish from a rusted biscuit tin box, she stomps to the backyard, alarming the cats. Sifting through the pots, she places one on the fire; stripping the yellow mahua flowers to their usable core, she throws in the dried sugar-rich petals, stirring with anger as the flames leap up around the cauldron. She can't just sit and watch the Naxals and police play with the villagers' lives. She had to do something, even if it was making mahua. Throughout its history, the precious mahua liquor has been periodically banned, restricted, accepted as pay-off by the army and the police or stolen and snatched by Naxals. She feeds wood to the fire, throwing in the bark and stirring the mahua pot, stirring till she becomes breathless. She hardly cried even after getting married; she had no time to. She prefers drops of sweat beading her face rather than feckless tears.

As the mahua vapours rise from the open vats, Birsu's brother-in-law comes with a *sirhana* leaf cup and pours out some of the last of the old mahua for himself. The man— who, though a man, has no resistance—is sometimes seen chanting spells as a *gunia*[8] to ward off evil spirits from his patients. But mostly, he is seen with a bottle, drinking deeply, for, he says, you need courage to sit by and watch things happen.

Birsu's own desire to drink the homemade hooch is fraught; each sip that she kisses lulls her mind, and at the same time, boils her anger. Her first sip is a gargle: sterilizing. The second divulges the aromas. By the third, she forgets about her swollen knee inflicted by the *green uniformed* woman, the noisy children who make enough noise to scare wild animals away and/or even the young girl who was taken away by the Naxals.

Birsu is not worried about Naxals, even though she worries about everything. They are young boys and girls, probably jobless and recruiting girls and boys from the neighbouring villages.

She is worried that fewer and fewer mahua trees grow wild. They often die too young.

She is worried about the numerous storms this year that killed them.

She is worried about the miners of the giant companies, which her husband says are not too far away. They will come up into her hills and kill the jungles, on which they depend on for everything, when they are finished in the valley. Even the police are powerless before them.

Overhead is the thinning moon. A deer comes down for the discarded leaf cups and then disappears behind a tamarind tree near the stream. Across the water comes the screech and clatter of small scarlet birds with black heads, passing on their way to somewhere colder, somewhere larger, somewhere better than here.

Radha is inside, singing herself to sleep. When she was born six years ago, she was beautiful, small and fragile. Her brown skin and dark big eyes made her stare seemed to be radically attuned. When Birsu first lifted her, she felt the pure tenderness of a baby, but in Radha's eyes was a vibrating desire to take form. The activist from Ramakrishna Mission insisted she had intelligent eyes meant for school: 'She will be a teacher or even a doctor.' The closest residential school was an hour away, in Orchha. There is no girls' school in the village, only an *anganwadi*.[9] The activist had given her the residential school's form. Birsu watches its pages flutter on the floor, held down by the weight of a pebble. She had practised her signature, taught to her by the activist, on a paper bag several times already. If she goes to the residential school, Birsu contemplates with the blue pen in her fist, Radha would grow away from them and their village. She would never go to a ghotul.

At her age, many springs ago, Birsu was in a ghotul.

* * *

Birsu was born in a village near Antagarh,[10] north of Narayanpur, in Chhattisgarh. In her village, when the night fell, men gathered in a circle under a tall mango tree. They exchanged news, weighed up the work done in the fields; but when they exhausted all these topics, they always opened a bottle of mahua. Every man had something to say about the mahua he'd once had in Kondagaon or in that village of Babu Kohaka, and the mahua that he would perhaps have again. The men reminisced about the mahua that was had at a death ceremony, or a birth ceremony, at a festival, or offered by their son-in-law's family; they described its floral scent and sharpness and recited songs or litanies in its honour.

Soon, drums would be beaten, and at their sound, the married men retreated home while the young and the unmarried prepared for the ghotul: a sort of clubhouse for boys and girls somewhere near the edge of each Maria village. Some of the boys went directly to the ghotul, while a few others went to the girls' houses to fetch them. A large hut with a fenced courtyard under the spreading branches of a giant banyan, the ghotul is a place embedded in and nurtured by the larger socio-religious landscape of the Gond society.

At home, a thirteen-year-old Birsu had already finished husking the grain, anointing the floors with fresh cow dung and making dal with pork. Her younger sister, Kariya, ran out to her as the drums went off and Birsu began dressing for the ghotul; she opened her braids, fluffing her hair into a beautiful dark cloud.

Only a few years ago, Birsu played the pretty game of *atoi mal-mal* with Kariya; girls from their neighbourhood would go around in a circle and smooth and part each other's hair, singing, 'Make my hair soft and mal-mal.' She now had no time for Kariya; she had changed. She walked with an extra swing in her hips, took too much time in the forest and brought too little wood. On most nights, she waited for a boy from the ghotul behind the door. The moment he'd arrive, Birsu would run back. It didn't matter that she had already been waiting in the patio, waiting for a silhouette to appear in the dark. Kariya, as a part of the daily act, would be the one to bellow, 'He's here for you', 'He's here for you,' as though she were the *usir* bird, bringing the first joyous tidings.

With her hand in her chin, Kariya looked enviously at her beautiful sister. She had a shapely nose, a pendulous lower lip and brown skin that glittered in the sun. Kariya, though, was named thus because she was born black: darker than the crow.

Birsu opened a tin of scented powder she had bought that day when they went to sell gourds and wild tomatoes from their field at the Antagarh weekly market. The barter system is still the traditional method of exchange among the Marias. Often, precious goods, like a bag of chironji, are sold to traders for a fistful of salt; or a bottle of mahua is traded for talcum powder. With her exaggerated white skin and chin tattooed with traditional symbols, Birsu looked like a child who had put on her mother's makeup—or one who was endeavouring to look older. She carefully applied some mahua oil and twisted her hair into a bun with a *fita*. Now that spring was here, she could decorate her hair with marigolds, velvety red *silyari* flowers and the new wooden comb.[11] The act of giving combs to express desire was an age-old tradition in the ghotul.

'Where did you get that comb from? It is not mother's,' Kariya pestered her, knowing fully well a boy at the ghotul gave it to her.

'What business is it of yours?' Birsu scowled.

Kariya sighed. 'When will I go to the ghotul, sister?'

'Oh, don't worry. I will take you months before you get your *phulsundari*,' Birsu consoled her, referring to the 'blossoming of the flower' or her first period. While most girls of her village went to the ghotul around ten years of age, Birsu had refused to go, pretending that her menarche,[12] or the first period, wouldn't stop. After a month, the head of the ghotul cajoled the petrified Birsu there. The *ladkaman,* or the boys at the ghotul,[13] on seeing her, snickered, '*Chi*, don't touch me, you are still dirty.' And another had mocked, 'Your pot had a hole in it, but today it has mended. You fixed it with lac.' She refused to go the next day, but her mother pushed her out of the house. 'Ghotul is a Maria tradition,'[14] she'd said, and holding her by an arm, told her the Lakari story.[15]

'Once upon a time, there lived seven *motiaris* who knew nothing about lovemaking. One day, they went to gather leaves with a grandmother; the old lady climbed the tree and the girls looked up and saw her vagina. When she told them what it was for, they were so frightened that they left the vicinity of the ghotul and went to live far away in the jungle. Whenever they saw a man, they beat him up and drove him away.' The story proceeds through various adventures to the inevitable conclusion: 'Each of the girls was seduced by a sadhu, called Lakari, and became pregnant.'

In her green sari, which ended a little below her knees, glittering with sequins, Birsu had looked out of place as she walked out of the stark, dusty compound after the conversation with her mother. Walking down the path towards the ghotul, Birsu wondered, why must a girl suffer it all: *godan* (tattooing), *chodan* (intercourse) and *paidan* (child-bearing)?

Since the previous year, the fireflies have disappeared; people say they've drowned. Earlier, girls would string them around their necks; the boys would trap the live ones in glass jars and release them in girls' saris. Tens and thousands of them would flutter in unison in the jungle's night air, drunk-walking under the moonlight of Antagarh. But that night, in the dark forest, only the ghotul was pulsing with murmurs and music.

There once lived the heroic Lingo, the youngest of seven brothers and a charming musician of sorts, who refused to indulge the lusty advances of his six sisters-in-laws (much to the relief his brothers). His attention, as the legend goes, was absorbed by a little hut outside the village, which he had built for himself; its walls were made of fish scales and the roof of snakes and peacock feathers. Lingo played his eighteen musical instruments every night in this sanctum sanctorum, or the ghotul. Hearing the melodies, the young boys and girls of the village, filled with overpowering desire, crept up to his hut and started spending their nights there. Like Lingo, they would go back to their parents' home before dawn. His green-eyed brothers tried to slay him in more ways than one, but the 'pure' Lingo survived all these attempts, which turned him into a cult figure who is now worshipped as a phallic deity and the founder of the ghotul.[16]

Since the days of Lingo, every Maria village has had a ghotul where the young boys of the village, starting from their adolescent years, start pouring in at dusk after their work in the fields while the girls, after helping their mothers with chores and housework, join in soon after. Gossip and cowrie games are soon followed by music and dance, ending with the wilder sexual games.[17] The reason, the Maria say, that Lingo did not allow himself to be seduced by the very attractive and willing wives of his brothers is because he was busy with the ghotul, not only, let it be noted, by its erotic delights, but also by its songs, dances, discipline and fellowship, with a peculiar mixture of restraint and freedom in the relationship between the sexes.

Inside the Antagarh ghotul, the boys were practising on the *mandri*,[18] *nissan*[19] and *pitorka*[20] gongs around a firepit. Birsu hurried to sit with the girls around another pit; they were crushing the dried tobacco, picked from their backyards, into a fine powder and weeded out the still moist leaves. Their cowrie armlets tinkled as they worked.

'I saw Ramesh's eyes follow the swing of your hips.' Jhankai elbowed Birsu, who ignored her.

'Didn't he give you a comb yesterday?' she pressed.

Birsu looked up at Ramesh: Probably a little over twelve, with faint down for a moustache, busy with his pitorka. One side of his face had a gooey green paste on it; a ghotul boy had crept up on him from behind, plastering his face with cow dung to roars of laughter from the ghotul. The loincloth around his waist, though, was spotlessly clean; she'd heard from someone that he had made the pitorka gong himself, with carvings of a tiger and dancing little girls of the ghotul. The Marias seemed to admire hard work more than physical features in men. For girls, though, it was different. Her friend Jhankai had a flat nose, a fat face and a short neck. She could have made herself beautiful by magic, but for that she would have to go all alone in the middle of the night to fetch the charred bones of a barren witch who had died and been cremated on the same day, and bathe with that powder. Unsurprisingly, Jhankai let her flat nose and short neck be.

'He took me to the forest yesterday,' Birsu finally whispered, breaking into a smile.

'Oh, you sly one.' Jhankai giggled. 'Did you tell the *belosa*?' she says, referring to the head girl of the ghotul.

Birsu shook her head, looking away as she thought of his arm on her waist while they drank mahua he had stolen from his home; they had sat on the forest floor, aroused by the violet and yellow flowers of *bilpat* that were considered weeds in his fields.

'Are you okay?' he'd asked as they walked to the forest, hearing her teeth rattle despite the warm sun.

When he finally stopped and turned towards her, they were in a patch of shade, surrounded by larger bushes and some trees. If Birsu's mind said 'run', her body argued 'stay'. But what if she got pregnant? When she first attended ghotul, she had changed her partner within a week because she was scared of him, as he had attempted to touch her in the night. The Marias claim that intercourse rarely takes place in the ghotul, and often, a girl or a boy would have intercourse years after joining the ghotul. Either the girl is too scared, or the boy is too young.

Ramesh asked her why she was standing so far away. He got close when she didn't, and he gave her a comb with a carving of a couple in coitus. Their eyes met and they both laughed.

They sat close together. Her palm touched his hand, both sweating. Birsu's whole body shivered with excitement. He told her old tales about flowers and grass. Minutes later, they were half naked, their hands going exactly where hands shouldn't have gone—or exactly where they should have.

Birsu looked around the ghotul while crushing the dried tendu. Most boys had the coarse, pimply particularities of adolescence: the still-childlike bodies with baby fat lodged in their cheeks, the unpractised rituals of grooming, the eagerness yet wariness of early sexual interaction. Imitating the older boys, they announced that they would like to indulge in 'surta': a longing for tobacco after a hard day in the fields. The head of the boys, who was already engaged to a girl in another village and living his last days in the ghotul, opened his new *dudo mori gota* or the breast-shaped tobacco bag, complete with motifs that resembled the pimples around the nipples of a woman's breast. The girls looked at it aghast, petrified, surprised, and then began to giggle. Most of these girls also had chubby cheeks, and often, as a lot of Maria woman did, small breasts and hips that seemed perky and highly charged.

This 'children's republic'[21] usually had the village panchayat as its ultimate head; while the girl members of the ghotul were called motiaris, the boy members were *cheliks*; their leaders were called belosa and *siredar* respectively. The girls would have to sanitize the floor with cow dung and clean ashes from the previous night, while the boys were in charge of the roofs and fences; any laxity in the duties led to consequent punishment. Both boys and girls were to be clean, oiled and dressed in their finest attire.

The Maria ghotuls weren't exactly wimpy while doling out punishments; they made the children stand on one leg for hours. Whipping their backs was customary. After the midnight fire was extinguished, the boys slept at the ghotul every night until they were married. The girls usually slept there too, but many resisted this heatedly, insisting they return home around midnight. In any case, all ghotul members went home by dawn.

'Where is our tobacco? You still haven't filled our leaf pipes?' one of the cheliks complained as the belosa hurried the girls with the tobacco.

'Not any more,' the siredar said, haughtily. 'It is too late. It is time for the ghotul *band atu*,[22] time to sleep.'

The belosa hastily instructed the girls to massage the boys instead, in an attempt to amend the situation; the attached girls approached their cheliks, and the unattached drew closer to the boys they liked. In theory, it was the girls, who were fewer in number compared to the boys, considering they got married earlier, who chose the boys by approaching them to massage or comb them and ultimately, sleep on their *dera*, their sleeping mats.

But in truth, it was a boy who often rejected a girl: the swagger expected by them from the other boys. Although it called for a fine for misbehaviour, a certain respect was accorded to a boy with many refusals to his credit. The ghotul, as a community, had a wider responsibility of preventing passionate love affairs, as that increased the likelihood of an unwanted pregnancy.[23]

'Birsu, you must massage Duma today. He has been asking you for some time now,' the *belosa* whispered. Birsu's eyes were focused on the floor, as though she was following caterpillar patterns on the mud. The tutelary belosa seemed to know that Ramesh and Birsu had paired yesterday; sleeping with a partner too often was fined in the ghotul, sometimes leading to expulsion from it, an idea feared by the young boys and girls.

Duma, an older boy at the ghotul, was tall and thin, unlike Ramesh, and his name translated to 'dead' in Halbi, to depreciate his value in the eyes of the hostile, hungry spirits that lived in trees. In the mornings, he worked in his father's grocery shop; in the evenings, when women started appearing at the ghotul, he would do push-ups on the rock outcrops like a lizard. He had been pursuing Birsu for weeks, making her wooden clips and buying glucose biscuit packets from Orchha.

While the *belosa* awaited her reply, Birsu saw a new entrant to the ghotul massaging Ramesh's neck from the corner of her eyes. There was a light pause, and a sigh, before Birsu said yes for Duma.

She began the massage with great vigour, kneaded his neck, arms and shoulders. Then it grew gentler, until her hands only caressed, roused affection and stirred, with every gesture, a new desire. She pulled out a comb from her hair and dressed Duma's into neat tufts. She slowly brought the comb to his back, and then took it to the stomach and lower. The younger girls followed seduction tips from the older girls, while the boys practiced cool new tricks learnt from their peers. Soon, Birsu joined Duma on his mat. From another corner of the ghotul, she heard the belosa fining Jhankai with logs of firewood[24] for laughing too loud.

Prenuptial sexual freedom isn't unusual among primitive tribes around the world. In Pottuna, New Guinea, unmarried girls are perfectly free to receive their lovers at night in their parents' houses. The favoured boy waits until the house is quiet, and the fire low; he slips into the house, and then unmarried girls and boys are allowed to act very much as they please in regard to their sexual relations. Abstinence, except when ceremonially imposed on the man, is practically unknown, and the girls are habitually polygamous. However, it is etiquette for the boy to retire quietly before daylight. Among the Uritoi of Polynesia, men and women have live-in agreements without marriage. So do the Igorots of the Philippines.

In the small, crowded ghotuls, siblings often slept in the same room with their respective lovers. How did the couples romance, then, let alone practise sexual intercourse (note: incest, even among cousins, was barred, and if it occurred, was dismissed after a fine)?

In the beginning, the couples slept on the mat, as brothers do with sisters, and once their hormones kicked in, things went further and the young adults followed their sexual instincts as easily as hunger. 'The setting was romantic—cozy, fire-lit huts, the stillness of the night, perhaps a moon, the bright fire in the courtyard, the tinkling bells tied to cheliks' waists and songs of the motiari could not fail to make their hearts beat faster. Everyone is lit by the golden glow of the fire; as music fills the air, and couples get closer and move into the hut and different corners of the ghotul; 'the superb light of cleopatrine passion was absent but so was the harsher gaze of excited grasping, lust.'

In this soft, diffused glow of affection, boys and girls lived together in that dormitory for years; a charming mixture of learning and experimenting with lovemaking, none of it meant to be taken seriously.

Birsu had pulled out her pubic hair with the help of ash and worn flowers in her hair not for a specific boy, but for all boys, and for the ghotul's honour and delight. The boys wore feathers in their hair and drummed, not to please a specific lover but to excite and gratify the entire ghotul. But mostly, they fell in love and out of it; coveted other cheliks' partners; arranged to meet girls in forests; played, sang and danced in the ghotul.

If nothing else worked, there was the most usual method of attaining arousal, found among various kinds of animals, from insects to birds to man—that is, some form of dance. Girls moved their hips in the dance, weaving through the rows of boys, which they often practise at the ghotul before festivals, weddings, death and other ceremonies. 'The Maria believe in the primordial authenticity of lust; it does you good; it's healthy and beautiful; when performed by the right people (such as a chelik and a motiari who are not cousins) at the right time (outside the menstrual period and avoiding forbidden days), sex is great fun; it's the best of the ghotul games; it's the dance of the genitals; it is ecstatic swinging in the arms of one's beloved. It ought not to be too intense; it must not be degraded by passiveness or defiled by jealousy, when partners change.'[25]

In reality, though, things were often different. By the time a young boy or a girl had spent long hours in the fields, deboned fish, collected logs, cared for younger siblings, lovemaking was imaginable, desirable, hormonally induced, but not necessarily acted upon.

Birsu was quick to realize that 'love' in ghotul could be a euphemism. That night, Duma held her a little too hard by her shoulders when she hesitated to accept his love.

She turned her head slightly to the side, as if it were an act of detachment or objectivity. Angered, he spat and swore, '*Madarchot*.'[26] She then let go, not like someone who is submitting herself in love, but someone whose mind lets their body go to run away from it.

'Nashamaina![27] I may be pregnant,' Jhankai whispered, as if talking to herself. The blue haze had not yet been dispelled by the rising sun as the girls got back home the next morning.

Birsu stared at her in horror and ushered her behind an abandoned hut.

'But how . . .? Oh, did you practise it during the taboo period?' she exclaimed, referring to the period immediately after menstruation, which the Maria considered the most fertile period, during which women were barred from coming to the ghotul as a contraceptive practice.[28]

When Jhankai shook her head, Birsu raised her eyebrows sardonically. Jhankai's lower lip started trembling and seconds later, she was crying with loud gasps that sounded like choking. 'I had prayed to the Nhani Kanyang (bathing maiden) at my first menstruation with eggs and coconuts, prayed that my blood flows by the moon during my time at the ghotul and I do not conceive. But what did I do wrong,' she sobbed, looking away from Birsu, 'that such doom fell upon me?'

A herd of boars had sleepily looked up as though they wanted to comment, but out of innate gentleness, refrained.

Revealing the ghotul's secrets through a pregnancy harmed the solidarity of the ghotul. So Jhankai was first administered an abortive mixture of gur, ashes of sal and some fresh mahua by the belosa that evening, whose salty language bore the sharp, poetic voice of tradition.

'Behaving like rabbits . . . you had slept with him three times[29] already. I had told you to change your chelik . . .' she hissed, pertaining to the Maria belief that the constant change of partners rendered conception less likely.[30]

When the abortifacient failed, the matter was taken to the panchayat. The boy from another village, whom Jhankai's parents had considered for her betrothal, was summoned, along with the chelik. The sarpanch, while chewing on a stalk, stood up to survey the horizon, as if contemplating, and then sat down again, cursing the slowness of the boars and the stupidity of chelik and motiari.

'The omens seem good. The usir bird on that sal tree seems to be singing well.' It was decided then that when the betrothed was willing to have Jhankai and accept the child, a fine would be imposed on the chelik, who seemed to have impregnated different women thrice already. A pregnancy among the Maria was dreaded because the routine of the daily life was upset, the matrimonial arrangements were disturbed and everyone made a fuss. But it was forgotten without much protest, whereupon things in the village sank back into a rather boring peacefulness. The world of the Marias would once again become gentle, kind—beige, as it were—as if nothing were a problem, really, and one might as well adapt or be left behind.

As a peer group, the ghotul was obliged to provide its service for weddings as well as occasions like deaths, road repairs and other odd jobs. For deaths, the Maria boys dug graves in their fields or near the streams (unless a person died of witchcraft, in which case he should be burnt), fed the grave mahua while the girls cooked feasts and danced—a tad bit more sombre than the one they danced, at, say, Jhankai's wedding.

For Jhankai's wedding, the teenage boys and girls, dressed in all their finery with beads and plumed headgear, danced all night; breaking every now and then to sip *salphi* from leaf cups. Boys in their peacock feather turbans and girls with their swan-like necks moved in and out of the circle. For almost a week, they prepared for the wedding: Boys hunted the meats, erected the tents; girls made the leaf cups and plates for the feast and brewed liquor for the wedding party.

On the day of the wedding, Jhankai was slathered with turmeric and given a bath by the motiaris while the cheliks fanned her. Her combs, the sign of youth, her love from cheliks and the ghotul, were stripped off her. Though her wedding was to be strictly a perfunctory ceremony (blame the pregnancy), the standard long *bidai* ceremony, or ceremonies, every evening at the ghotul as boys and girls sang songs, was not compromised upon.

'This will be your home till tonight,' they sang.

'It was filled with your presence

But now the house is silent.

You came here at sunset

In your hand a broom
You went to clean the ashes at the ghotul
Like a peacock dancing
You had a boy lover
But now you leave him behind, alone and sad
You are going away
You were living in the kingdom of the unmarried
You will never enter it again.'

'Oh, oh.' Jhankai burst into streaming tears. Never had anyone seen anyone bawl that way, tears pouring down her face, trailing to her ears, and spattering on to her chest as though it were a pool of water. There was a moist eye here, or another there, amongst the cheliks too.

Secretly, Birsu knew, while wiping her own tears, that these were tears of relief. Her happy life at the ghotul was soon to be replaced by the drudgery of marriage, but who knew better than the Marias, whose sexual appetite has been dulled after the ghotul, that what they look forward to is a sense of permanence, a home of their own and a relationship that will be recognized forever? In the ghotul, the partner always belonged to someone else.

'Give food and water to your husband's parents
Fight with them not, don't upset them
You will live happily, or your life will crumble
Live happily, with husband's younger brothers and sisters
Pick your vegetables from the forest, fetch water, bring them wood, clean their house
Yesterday you laughed and played with us; tomorrow laugh and play with them.'

With hardly any sexual diseases and a stronger sense of domestic morality and conjugal fidelity, the Marias seem to look forward to living a happy life after marriage. They look forward to spouses with a gentle, more dedicated approach to marriage. It is only by the breach of a rule that chelik and motiari choose their own spouse. Mostly, marriages were arranged by parents. Birsu's marriage, though, was an exception.

Come spring, when the harvests were complete, the tribes looked forward to the *cherchera punia* festival, when boys and girls together took long trips, or expeditions, to other villages, danced in the ghotuls of other villages they visited and slept there. Hosts and visitors entertained each other with songs and dance. In the night, after rounds of drinks, the stage was set for activity more intimate than dancing: choosing partners, massaging and so on. In the morning, the dancers wore masks, went around the village, and stood before homes, begging for the auspicious liquor, rice and pulses.

'*Mai kothi ke dhan la harhera . . .*'

'Come out, girls, and see they have come. They have come from the upper world. Give us our presents quickly, for it is growing very late. Tie up a pair of bullocks, kill a fat hen and bring rice out of the granary.'

On one such expedition, Sukaru had come to Birsu's village in Antagarh. Mesmerized by her beauty, he urged her to visit his village. '*Mere liye aana,*' he'd said. Maybe she had smiled at him; maybe she hadn't. As if reading from the pages of a courtship manual, he sat that night with a bottle of mahua under his arm, and she installed herself at his side for the rest of the evening.

Birsu's parents refused to let her go when she mentioned visiting Sukaru in his village. 'It is far, and, we hear, dangerous.' So she lied, and left on the pretext of an expedition.

A band of cheliks and motiaris left for Gudari, Sukaru's village in the Abujhmar hills; they walked with bundles of food and clothes on their head, stopping to fill themselves up with starch from the *doomar* tree[31] or boiling the rice and lentils they carried with them. It struck Birsu how different the landscape was from Usili, her village in Antagarh. The greenness burst here in thickets, unlike the tame trees of her hometown. It was here, in Orchha, near the Indravati river, that she had first seen the Maoists.

Within a small clearing near the foothills of Abujmarh, a group of men stood with guns on their backs. Their thin frames and features were burnt out by depredations of the sun.

Kamlu, a motiari with their troupe, muttered under her breath, 'Be still. They can't see us yet.'

One of the men held a young boy by his collared shirt and slapped him methodically. 'Are you the police informant? Tell us, are you?' The boy stared back at them, blank, his knees giving away with each slap. Seconds later, they shot him. Chanting Maoist slogans, they disappeared into the deepening green of the jungles.

Birsu wanted to run behind them and ask them why they had killed the boy. But that would sound senseless. She didn't want to sound senseless, yet she didn't want to be a quiet little blossom. So she threw her bundle of clothes and the pot full of rice on the floor.

A chelik was the first to move, leading the way minutes later, sticking to a trodden path to make less noise. 'In the name of mining,' he whispered, 'the government is taking away the lands of the forest people. They give them work of making roads and other odd jobs, wads of cash, alternative housing in other villages nowhere close to the forest—in return for their land and their departure. So a lot of these men, even women and children, I hear, have joined the Naxals coming in from Andhra for self-rule. The police often bribe these villagers to show them the tracks the Naxals were using.' But the hills and forests here had no tolerance for excessive bravado.

Birsu was surprised. She did not know things in Bastar had come to this; in Usili life was blinkered, the news unreal, functioning only as fodder for evening talks or for outbursts of drunken men. For Birsu, her sense of soul and livelihood was inextricably linked to the forest, and the bait of money that development seemed to offer held little attraction. Whatever she needed that the jungles could not give—biscuits, salt, oil, talcum, sugar—she could exchange for its goods in the village markets.[32]

Later that evening, the boys of their little Antagarh party helped the ghotul members of Gudari create a straw bed on which the dead boy would be carried; they dug a grave near the stream in the jungles and buried his body and painted his tomb in bright colours.

According to the Maria custom, at every important or less important occasion in the dead man's family, its spirits would be called upon and implored: to protect a newborn child, bless a marriage, keep famines away, ensure good rainfall, protect the crop or bring success in hunting and fishing. The dead needed just a burial, Birsu thought, but the living would ask and ask.

The dense forests of Abujhmar have long been isolated with the Indravati river segregating it from Bastar region. During the British rule in India, Abujhmar remained in isolation and constitutionally 'excluded'. After the Independence of India, its isolation continued, except when in 1958, the government refugees from East Bengal came in. Later, the hills started getting exploited for their mineral wealth and the uneducated, backward tribals were exploited by prevalent feudalism.

The Maoists, or the communist radicals, had first arrived in the thickets of Abujhmar in the 1980s from the neighbouring state, formerly known as Andhra Pradesh, escaping an ambush by policemen. Just when Maoist leaders had thought that their demand for an egalitarian government had disintegrated into smaller Naxal groups, Adivasis, here in the hills, readily welcomed the armed insurgents from Andhra. The Naxals would help them demand freedom for their like: the peasants and the forest dwellers: the new victims of the rampant mining who were fast losing their livelihood, the forest, for which depended on for everything. This mineral rich region is home to open coal pits, where massive quantities of the carbon rock are still mined and, in turn, the forest residents offered all sorts of compensation to the locals—jobs, money, alternative housing—in return for their land and their departure. While many have accepted this, for others, like Birsu and her villagers, their forests and lands are everything to them.

The Maoists made their home in this 35,000 square miles of jungle, one of the last of India's unmapped territories, recruiting those who were harrowed by their homes being cracked by the shockwaves from machines in the mines, and their lands snatched for further mining. The hills started becoming a dangerous mesh of explosives: those of the mines and then the landmines and bombs used by the Naxalites to kill police and soon after, the security forces like CRPF retaliating with bloody 'encounters' and burning their encampments, often killing many of the innocent. The losers of this massacre were the 'suspected government informers' who were tried in people's courts and hung on trees or the 'Naxal protectors' who spent weeks in police prisons, leading to a massive swell in the homicide rate, nowhere in the official figures, of more than 15,000 deaths in the last twenty-five odd years.

Later that night, in Gudari, Birsu and her party were greeted by the sound of the nagadas, which, in their festive fervour, refused to go sombre in spite of the death of a ghotul member ('it's a common occurrence around here'—

an elderly had refused to accept their condolence offerings, in fear of disappointing the festive gods). Preparations had been made for the 'dance'. Young boys and girls assembled one by one, while elders squatted around the fire drinking mahua. The boy who died, like many others who had been dying in the past months, was briefly discussed and then quickly forgotten.

After a week in Gudari, Birsu became Sukaru's motiari, but refused to accept his love. Their troupe stayed in the Gudari ghotul for a few days, but soon, Birsu longed to go back home to Antagarh, where the ghotul conversations mostly revolved about fields, mahua or a motiari's half-day disappearance in the jungles. Here, the boys seemed older, less playful. They were either frustrated with the CRPF for forcing them to make roads and camps or were busy avoiding conscriptions by the Maoists.

Besides, Birsu was not yet done with the ghotul life and enjoyed the immediate pleasure and companionship-especially dancing and travelling to different villages. Behind Sukaru, she feared, lurked a husband.

A sirhana, or a shaman, was approached by the love-stricken Sukaru, and after much chanting, his ancestors spoke through the sirhana medium, suggesting some ashes be offered to the deities, be mixed with rice and given to Birsu.

'She then will never leave you,' the sirhana said, his eyes rolled in head while his body heated up. He was even put on a meat diet of the virile organs of a goat. When Birsu still insisted she leave with her troupe back to Antagarh, Sukaru pulled the last trick out of the bag. '*Sarus pite joridar*'—two cranes make a perfect pair, he told himself. On the order of a sirhana, he pursued a pair of sarus cranes. They usually moved in pairs. When one died, the other quickly followed suit. One of them was caught by Sukaru; he then slipped some liquor down its throat. Next, the bird was burnt; its vestiges tied in a little bundle around Sukaru's waist.

The next evening, as Sukaru sat in the ghotul, discreetly fondling the ash bundle on his waist, a warm feeling blossomed within Birsu. Out of the many, he was hers, she thought, while singing with other girls around the fire, and this simple recognition was enough to endear him to her. The boys at the ghotul maybe more exciting, but she could hardly depend on them. In a while, Sukaru too forgot his usual reserve and danced with uninhibited, clumsy exuberance. Flushed with optimism, mahua and affection, Birsu agreed to marry him. The next day, Birsu was wedded to Sukaru, without the presence of her parents, and she moved to Gudari, forever.

\* \* \*

Just when she is going to sign the school form, Birsu's neighbour appears at the door. 'Krishna was not eaten by them. She has been returned by the Maoists. She is back . . .' she huffs. Birsu hurries to the ghotul to see the girl, but finds her at the edge of the village. A small group of people stand around her, staring at her dirty hands and face; she is dressed in men's clothes—green pants and a shirt. Birsu's throat dries up; she reminds her of the Mao woman she had seen in the forest yesterday.

The story of what happened is recapped, in fractional, fragmented versions that alters, depending upon who is asking: a CRPF man, or a woman with notepad. But it is only when the women of the village are alone, the girl tells the whole truth. Birsu listens on, as she describes in broken sentences: 'Me and two girls from the ghotul, Kariyu and Gowri were leaving the ghotul around midnight when they caught hold us of. The other girls escaped. The men, they were expanding . . . army'—she says, sitting on a rock, staring at a faraway distance. They spoke in loud Gondi, winked at young girls outside the ghotul, and said—'Come with us for a better life.'

'One of the boys'—she chokes—'looked as old as the ghotul boys but had dirty fingers and face of the rat. Impressed by my wood-chopping strength, he carried me on his shoulders into the forest . . . afterwards, he said he loved me and laying his sweaty head . . .,' she says, wiping her tears, 'on my bare chest, he told me he too was abandoned like me—he was an urchin—though it was harder for him, for he had been an urchin for many years—and he was not just a moawadi but a boy who had ached, and had seen horror and wanted now only to have babies with me . . . many children, mostly boys and some girls, too, yes, why not girls! And they would have an army of children to expand the Mao army, so his comrades would increase. He was gentle with me when we were alone, unlike the boys at the ghotul . . .'

The girl then looks up; rows of tears streak her dirty face. I must go look for him again. I must go back to him.'

To everyone's surprise, she gets up and runs back into the deep jungle. The women call after her, but she refuses to look back. Shaking their heads, the women return home in groups of two or three. Birsu continues to stand at the edge of the forest, waiting to see if her silhouette forms back under the trees, if the she changes her mind and comes back to the village.

Later that night, Birsu is feeling the school admission paper between her fingers when Sukaru comes back home. She does not look at him while narrating Krishna's return back to the Maoist who stole her from the village.

Sukaru continues changing into his vest, as if there is no need to feel any sympathy at this news. 'Make me food early tomorrow. A new officer has been posted and is still enthusiastic about coming early to work.'

'We will not send Radha to the ghotul. Let her go to school,' Birsu tells Sukaru. He looks up at her, surprised. Shrugging his shoulder, he walks out of the hut to fix a leak in their tin-covered roof. Like Birsu, he does not think hard about things and fight his way through the darkness. 'She may then become a police officer, or teacher,' she tells after him, or even a Mao, she whispers to herself.

# 5

# THE KHASIS OF SHILLONG

*Two sisters face the burden of what other women in the world covet—a matrilineal society*

Shillong, Meghalaya

Shillong's traditional market Iewduh is a honeycomb of narrow lanes packed with tiny shops, each specializing in a different thing—dried fish, cane baskets, turmeric and garam masala. Jars of honey and bamboo pickles beam through the grey smog floating on the streets. The streets are strewn with apples, pineapples, betel leaves, various parts of the pig and wriggling silkworms that are, apparently, quite delicious once fried in oil. Every store spills a different scent into the cold, suffocating air. Two or three attendants, mostly tribal hill women, man these stalls in the traditional *jainsem*,[1] their sunburnt faces looking at the passers-by.

In one of the many home-style Khasi restaurants,[2] a now all-too-common scene takes place. A man with a presumably Bengali accent asks for *jadoh*—rice cooked with pork and blood. When a hill girl brings it along, the man looks at the rice and immediately calls out, 'Aye', but the girl keeps going, so the man raises his hand and repeats loudly, 'Ayee!' Everyone besides the waitress turns to look at him. She's gone. After several minutes, she comes back from wherever she's been hiding.

With a tone of great patience, he asks, 'What is this, please?'

'It's what you ordered.'

'But there is hardly any meat. I had ordered jadoh.'

'That's what you've got.' The girl opens her mouth to tell him that he was expecting a biryani, not a jadoh, but her resolve fails. She stares at Iewduh beyond him, at a future without these immigrants.

Outside, crowds walking through the drizzle are more diverse than ever before; tribesmen from hills nearby drag their produce in bamboo baskets, flattening the garbage heaped in piles; shop owners—mostly Marwaris—haggle with them, and many a times a matron, a Bengali with a large red bindi, comes in on her way back from work, carefully examining the slivers of fish to cook for her children. Then comes a rare sight, and then, an even rarer one.

First, a mother of a certain age—perhaps a grandmother—tall, in crumpled, dusty sari, with a hijab. Then, second, a young woman in the same colouring, stupendously and strikingly dressed in an embroidered burkha, with her two babies, their noses runny, hanging by her sides. Even for the cosmopolitan Shillong, a covered woman would have been someone who had come from outside, say, a tourist. For half a minute, the two women inadvertently walk in step, and then suddenly, looking at cops poking their batons through the wares of hill women, disappear into a lane with a glide of the black edifice, leaving billowing orbs of hazy, confusing grey. They are not sure of the geography of this foreign place; they don't know if the road that goes uphill is safer than the road that goes downhill, like the many cabs trying to find old addresses that the map does not recognize. They stand at the crossing, figuring out where to go next. The immigrants. And the tribesmen. They and the Bengalis, the Sylhetis, the Sikhs, the Marwaris, the Assamese and more.

Strangers, lost on a crossroads.

'The burkha-clad women are Rohingyas who fled from Burma,'[3] a shop owner tells a tourist in the gentlest of murmurs. He needn't speak in whispers, for his voice is barely audible over the numerous Altos honking on the streets. 'They come here looking for safety?' the tourist asks. This is a lie. 'They come here looking for opportunity,' says the shop owner. This is the truth.

When they arrived in the town, it must have been an unfamiliar place that was soothing to their senses. The landscape: green needles of leaves bunched together in pine trees and the proximity of freshwater fish in the Bara Pani. The smell: of wood smoke and apples; of food. The temperature: cold and windy, unlike the sticky humidity of their homelands. The possibility: of trade or even manual labour.

But if they had noticed the increasingly prolonged winters cracking the walls of bakeries; the disappearing pear trees giving way to people who needed to be accommodated; and as the sun set, shoppers rushing through the transactions before darkness fell, bringing with it the fearful images of violence and insecurity; they, then, might have turned back.

Wansuk and Syrpai Rynjah know better. The two women have been watching Shillong age for over eighty years now. From the window of their grey home on a slope beyond Iewduh their small figures watch through the frost. They look down at the two Khasi boys in jackets, standing near a bike, hooting at a Sardar in a turban in Khasi: 'Two more blows on that head, and you can wear a bigger bandage.'[4] They laugh raucously as the Sikh hastily disappears into an alley.

During the day, boys like these are a part of the lumpen elements[5] of varied unions, protesting the ouster of non-tribal traders in Iewduh. The newspapers said that today, a shop was pulled down in the market, its wares stolen and a few carts set slight. Every time the students mobilized their struggle, political tension intensified in Iewduh, turning it into a breeding ground for tribal versus non-tribal politics. The strikes would lead to closures, which meant the greatest hardships for the poor pavement sellers, which were, ironically, the tribal women who were struggling to raise children and had no savings.

The women sip their red tea by the window for a few more minutes, shivering as the light slowly changes and the pink cast of the dusk deepens, transforming the air of ancient sadness that hangs over the scene into an ordinary evening. Wansuk and Syrpai Rynjah, followers of the traditional Niam Khasi[6] religion, and sisters to each other, have lived together in their mother's ancestral home for years, peering down their window without hiding their disdain or curiosity, evening after evening, and teacup after teacup.

'The tea is too dark,' Wansuk complains in thick Khasi-laced English, her mouth slightly crooked from ageing.

Her voice is soft and dry; the words decipherable only to her sister.

'You should have made it yourself then,' Syrpai says, bristling. They both have grey hair that is frizzy, forcefully pulled back into buns; tattooed eyebrows sit atop the wrinkled eyes. Their cheekbones protrude like the tops of two peaches, the ones that every Khasi grandma gets as though it were a part of the race's evolution.

'These boys should be put behind the bars. Is this what that church teaches them?' Wansuk clucks her tongue. 'It is definitely not what the Khasi sermons prescribed to us.'

Syrpai smiles sideways, although it's also a smile that could serve as firm punctuation to Wansuk's statement— that is, a silent request to end it. Isn't old age supposed to have a satisfying end to the twisted arc of life, she wonders? Assimilating their experiences and sorting them into neat little boxes. But in this, Syrpai forgets that they, the old people, are victims of ailments, both mental and physical, not to mention accident, impulse, and ill luck, just as anybody else; just as chaotic, just as ungrateful.

Shillong had started showing xenophobic tendencies after Meghalaya was carved out of Assam as a separate state in 1972. Most of the Khasis had converted to Christianity over the last few decades; immigrants were taking over the markers and Shillong stopped being what it once used to be. Before this, their families had histories that were understood by their friends, shared by their neighbours; doors were open all night without any fear.

Last year, when Wansuk protested about Bible readings at public schools, she was abused on the street outside her house. When she cried out, the assailant put a hand on her mouth with such force that nearly all her teeth, which were old and brittle, were crushed to dust.

'See, this is what you get for sitting up and overusing your brains,' Syrpai had told her at the dentist's as Wansuk sat in the chair, with too many of the doctor's tools in her mouth to protest the accusation. 'Soon you'll become an irksome oldster like that Careen, or that lonesome man Samuel, telling people off on the streets.'

Inside, their tube-lit home seems to have been carefully put together over the years: black-and-white family portraits, traditional cane baskets and mats hanging on the walls; plenty of souvenirs like hand-woven silk sofa slips and porcelain dolls are displayed in the living room along with bottles of medicines and jars of local herb concoctions.

Syrpai puts her red tea-filled cup on the table where the cup ring gnaws into the table polish, and older sister Wansuk immediately rubs it with her napkin. Her false teeth are too big for her mouth. She removes them, setting them down in a bowl of water. They were bought last year after the attack.

'This bit about being nostalgic about horse-drawn carriages on empty streets and the gracious bungalows of Englishmen before the immigrants came pouring in is nonsense. I long for the simple Khasi before the British looted him of his heritage and identity,' she spits out.

Wansuk and Syrpai's grandmother loved to tell them, and they loved to hear, the story of the evil British officer David Scott. In the early 1800s, he simply strolled into Khasi and Garo hills and saw plenty of opportunity to extend his colony by exploiting the tribal simpletons. Inadvertently, he extended a road into the hills after gaining control over local rebels. Their grandmother's grand-uncle was allegedly one of the rebels who threw down the gauntlet by offering *shohnoh*, or his son's blood, to the indigenous snake demon god U Thlen.[7]

'Was he released later?' Syrpai tries to recall.

'Only when he converted to Christianity,' Wansuk hisses.

The sisters like to show an old map of Shillong[8] to anybody who is willing to see: the rivulets, streams and short walks that took one to the grassy plains and forests and a green patch called the Mawkhar region, in the present north Shillong constituency, their childhood home. Back then, their house was on a stretch of path that went up to a stream, where the road towards the polo ground is now. Wansuk, her brother and few others, no taller than the pineapple shrubs, would ascend the incline, chasing one another until they reached a stream where they washed their clothes. Leaving the clothes on a rock, they'd wander around, losing themselves in the forests with no markers, indicators or landmarks. They knew the trees and the shrubs and bushes, and this creeper that grew yellow flowers with red specks. They'd crush it in their fists and inhale its smell. It was said that these flowers purified the air. They are gone now. The pine trees, their symbols of abundance and nobility, are gone too. So are the hillocks.

The fields in those hills would grow potato now and mustard then. Since they flattened the land and fertilizers came in, they never wait for the land to heal. It goes from rice to more rice and then rice. How weary must be the field, destined to exist in the future, having existed in the past; though it was not always a field. It once used to be a forest.

When Wansuk was about eight, midwives rushed in to help her mother in labour. A girl was born. Now in an old-fashioned Khasi family, male babies are welcomed, but the birth of a girl calls for a feast. The entire Rynjah family cheered, 'The *khadduh* is born!' The Khasis follow the matrilineal principle of descent, residence and inheritance. The youngest daughter inherits, children take their mother's surname, and once married, the khadduh, or the youngest sister, and her husband live in her mother's home. This makes khadduh, what the non-Khasis would call, however incongruously, the 'man' of the house. The khadduh[9] is the custodian of the ancestral property and passes it on to her daughter. She also has a duty towards her brothers, sisters or her mother's brother, who may come to live with her in life or in extraordinary hardship, to take care and to house them.

The joy of Syrpai's birth, regrettably, was short-lived. As the midwife explained, the baby had got herself into a bit of a pickle and minutes after she was born, the mother was lost to the delivery. *'Tang shu kha ka kime ka, ka kmie ka lah pynkyrshah ia ka,'* the grandmother croaked with a smile when she first held the newborn Syrpai. Loosely translated, that meant when the mother died, she left her daughter with a traditional festive Khasi checked apron called a *jain kyrshah.* Just like dark bamboo barks fall away to reveal the tender bamboo shoot, the mother left her responsibility of being a khadduh on the little baby's shoulders. At the naming ceremony, while a baby boy was presented with a sword, a bow and three arrows, a baby girl would be given a conical basket, Ka Khoh, and a head strap meant for carrying loads, symbolizing that women are meant to bear the burden of the family.

Soon, the children learnt to name themselves, according to their roles in the families: While Syrpai was khadduh, her older cousins would be *bah,* equivalent to 'brother', but bah, her grandmother said, really meant 'the heart that walks ahead of me'. . . A brother was 'head' of the house, even as the khadduh and her husband took care of the ancestral property and the maternal family needs. The older sister, like Wansuk, meanwhile, would be *hymmen kynthei,* or the one who will pour the knowledge that she gains, taking up the responsibility of the family till she gets married.

By virtue of her gender, a kind of motherhood was thrust upon Wansuk: caring for her newborn sister and her father. Wansuk boiled water for their baths on sticks. When there were no more sticks, she'd collect them from the hillock. She changed sheets, chopped vegetables and never really slept in her bed. By the time their father returned, the pre-teen Wansuk was already asleep on the floor, with her baby sister in her arms.

Their father, a lab assistant, never remarried, but after work he sang to his bottle of rum.

'*Khu Blei, my love, ku Blei,*'[10] he mumbled, cuddling the bottle close to his chest.

Wansuk would sniff the air near her father when he was at the door. If he had tanked up, he seemed hollow, as if he were giving directions to his body from afar. She'd then quickly direct him to his room before her grandmother came out. Being a Khasi, her father had lived in his mother-in-law's home since his marriage. Now, while all the siblings had their father's stark cheekbones and strong colouring, everyone in Wansuk's maternal family was pinkly pretty and had grown plump. The grandmother, just like their mother, was beautiful, always poised and quaveringly defiant; her father, in contrast, seemed compliant and yielding. While their grandmother cooked for him, she univocally ensured the kids didn't turn out like him. She could tell, by the angle of the children's eyebrows, if they lied or fell short of duty. She saw through everything: closed eyes, doors, walls; she read minds too.

'Polish those teacups with vinegar before putting them back.'

'Oh, push that insolent hair back in your bun!'

'No dates on Sundays! You must go to the Seng Khasi hall for sermons.'

Seng Khasi was the organization formed to undo the non-tribal and British influences on the community.

Being a devout indigenous Khasi was supreme for the grandmother, and she had obdurate views about everything, especially matters of discipline. The children performed all their ancestral worships, and on Sundays, went to meetings of Seng Khasi.[11] With this unequivocal induction into life by a materfamilias,[12] the girls learnt to keep a home, study, perform ancestral worships, go for annual pilgrimages to heaven's navel[13] and take care of their father, however drunk he returned home.

A homemade safety test was administered to all the children in the house. On pertinent days, an egg was broken, and if it cracked completely open the first time, the girls would be grounded and made to sit beside the grandmother all day; the unbroken egg was an unmistakable sign that if they were permitted out, they would be lured by non-Khasi boys who would make them pregnant.

Those days, elders would tell their girls all manner of stories to keep them away from non-tribal males. 'Don't hold their hands, or they may transfer a spirit into you', or 'when you see them on the road, walk in a cross pattern before them to ward off trouble.'

In the hills, fatwas[14] by village durbars or NGOs aimed at restricting alliances between a Khasi woman and a non-Khasi man were neither new nor unusual. At the heart of the issue, rabidly gnawing at the tribe for decades, was the suspicion that an alliance between a Khasi woman and a non-Khasi man was a mere social contract that would allow the outsider male to exploit the tribal status of the

Khasi woman who inherits her family's fortune, especially, the khadduh.

Grandmother's egg remained stoic once in a while, and the girls would then skip school. On such evenings, their aunts would drop in. They'd together slice vegetables for pickling and later, sit with red tea and balls of fried rice dipped in jiggery.

'Iewduh seems to be getting smaller for our stalls,' an aunt would complain.

'Have you heard that Shylla is all set to marry a Bengali?' another would snort, speaking of their wayward cousin.

Soon, the evening would culminate with a few rounds of *phawar* [15] or folk rhymes that Khasis pass on orally from generation to generation. Their grandmother's favourite phawar was:

'*Dohkha ha nanpolok ki iabiej ia u shana
Da peit ho parari ioh phi biej ia u mama*'
(Fish at Ward's lake are crazy about chickpeas
Look my compatriots lest you are crazy like uncle)

The Khasi males always used the phrase *leit khwai* or 'to go fishing' when trying to court young girls. In this phawar, the word *dohkha* (fish) refers to young and naive Khasi girls who are at the very heart of the matrilineal system. Like the fish of Ward's Lake, a man-made water body commissioned by the British officer Ward, the girls can be easily lured and swept away by the false promises of love. The word 'uncle' here implies any non-tribal male. 'Stay away from the men of the plains and the British who'll ultimately leave us for the women of their own community,' their grandmother would tell the girls. And then squeezing her eyes shut, she'd pray into some rice and keep it in their pockets before they left home the next day. 'May He keep you away from all troubles,' she'd tell them at the door.

Back then, the East India Company seemed to have considered it their duty to 'redeem' the hill people of Khasi and Garo Hills who followed their traditional animistic[16] religion. The British dubbed them 'noble savages' and tried to confer upon them 'the blessings of the civilization' through Christianity. Evangelization among the Khasis was started in the early 1800s by Christian missionaries long before the occupation of the hills by the British government. Thomas Jones, the founder of the missions, was given the job of spreading education in the hills, but the biggest objective was to preach Christianity. Opposition to the schools by the locals commenced when young pupils refused to join animal sacrifices, venerating family spirits and eating raw meat, as was the custom of Khasis in those days. They cut their long hair, and covered their bodies.[17]

By 1864, the government assumed almost entirely the financial burden of educating the tribes. The Khasi women were eager to learn since the matrilineal system placed a heavy responsibility on women: the raising of their children. Within the next two years, the schools in the hills rose to seventy, with about 1316 pupils. Along with literature, medical missionaries also helped in the rapid progress of evangelization. Khasis were often victims of regular outbreaks of diseases such as cholera and small pox. Before the British, the tribesmen resorted to sacrifices to the spirits as remedial measures, which of course failed invariably and as a result, the members of the Lyngdoh clan, who propagated these sacrifices as medicine men, were soon discredited. The devastation caused by cholera was often so severe that the men finally succumbed to foreign medicines and vaccinations and soon, the mission gained a great deal of popularity. By the 1870s, people gradually ceased to regard Christian conversion as a *sang*, or taboo. The number of converts swelled to 514 by 1971. Today, about 80 per cent of Khasis are Christian converts.

Grandmother knew about the literature, medical missions and hygiene consciousness that the English brought to the hills, but for her, all this was a pointless prelude to the real story—the deviation of the people from their traditional reputation of simplicity and truthfulness. They ceased to regard their sacred groves and pools, traditional dances and festivals. The dead were buried instead of being cremated and the ancient *mawbynas*, or the memorial stones erected by people for their ancestors, were flattened; in their place came homes, markets and churches. When the colonizers stopped growing with convoy and the guns to impose their will, they brought out their cultural artillery—dances at Shillong Club, Golf Club, Pine Wood and Western movies at Kelvin and Garrison cinema halls. Young boys and girls swooned to Dame Vera Lynn, fondly known as the 'Forces' Sweetheart', when she came to

Shillong for a concert—the crowds loved it. But throw in traditional instruments like a *tangmuri* or a *duitara*,[18] the crowd's noise would drown them out.

As a quick remedial measure, the Seng Khasi elders pushed their young to dance at Weiking[19] Grounds for the Shad Shuk Mynsiem festival,[20] not only celebrating the arrival of spring and the sowing of seeds, but also reinstating faith in the Khasi philosophy of the matrilineal system. Men, both married and unmarried, danced with their swords and whips, donning the role of protectors of maidens. Only unmarried and virgin women, as a rule, were allowed to dance and they shuffled in the inner circles: bare-footed, moving forward or backward with their eyes cast downwards.[21]

Each year, Wansuk and Syrpai would dress in traditional family heirlooms of *rupa, sai khyllong* and *pansgiant* along with a *lasubon*, a silver attachment with flowers for their hair, and dance at the Weiking Ground. The silver crown on the virgin maiden's head was to honour the position of the woman in the society, a keeper of not only her honour, but the entire Khasi race.

The girls danced their hearts out, Wansuk especially. One watcher in the crowd told another, 'Did you see that girl dancing? So fluid!' And she'd wish dreadfully that her grandmother had been there. The remarkable thing was that even if she *was* there, she did not hear. Even if she did hear it, she'd pretend she didn't comprehend. Others learnt not to praise the girls, lest they spoil them. Even other people liked to please her grandmother.

One evening, the girls returned home from the festival along with a sea of yellow; they, and the other neighbourhood girls, were dressed in their turmeric-coloured festive gear and admiring each other's jewels when the girls saw their grandmother, standing red-faced at the door.

'That bastard of your father hasn't been home since last night. Go look for him in the market.'

Wansuk caught hold of her little sister's hand and looked everywhere: at the biscuit shop, or the man whom he usually drank with outside a bar and even inside the little room behind it, where he sometimes disappeared with the singers of the club.

It was nightfall. Their little feet had grown blisters from a long day at the grounds and all the searching when the girls saw him walking hand in hand with a woman, his new wife—Bethany. He was stroking her rounded pregnant belly. Bethany did not know about Wansuk and her sister, but bought them a slice of cake, even as their father half-pretended to know them. When the children walked back home, the clouds that had muffled the day like a fleece broke up and floated away like pink wisps in the sky; a thrush was joyous somewhere in a tree. Syrpai loved sitting in horse carts[22] and contemplated throwing a tantrum to sit on one, but after casting quick, buoyant, wary looks at her elder sister, she seemed to understand that this evening did not exist inside the envelope of ordinary time. At home, they sat with their grandmother and finished their dinner without leftovers. Syrpai ate less and then simply drew in her book: a tree, two mountains, three members of their home—the girls and their grandmother.

Wansuk was relieved. That was one less person to take care of: fewer sheets, fewer meals and no more frantic searches in the neighbourhood drinking shops. Until one day, their mother's brother came to live with them. Ribor was a lecher, often monkeying with women. He poured his alcohol into the meat. He came home not before eleven in the night and slept till noon. He didn't pray, never went to the Seng Khasi hall. When he entered the room, it was a little man whose face was wrinkled, as though someone had squished him between two weights; his bald head bore but a few strands of hair.

Ribor's wife had divorced[23] him because their physical intimacy was infrequent; he couldn't bear her children. Others said he had a propensity to sow wild oats; he often indulged in 'unofficial' polygamy. His wife went on to have a child outside wedlock, a common practice among Khasis as matrilineality protects women from social ostracism. If she chose to raise her children on her own, she was financially safeguarded with her inheritance from her mother.

In any case, Ribor was packed off to his mother's place with a shawl to tie around his neck and a bag of clothes, which were of no use because he mostly walked around the house wearing grey pyjamas and shabby slippers. He hardly shaved, and when he did, there was a grey shadow on his sunken cheeks.

One day, when the grandmother returned from the Seng Khasi hall, their uncle Ribor stood before the door. When he opened his mouth, he revealed a line of teeth decaying from the acidity in his liquor. He said, 'Do you still pray, mother?'

'Well . . .'

'To whom are you praying? To the God who made the British and gave jobs to everyone but the Khasis?'

'Why don't you get married again, Ribor?' grandmother sighed.

'Me? Half of me, if not more, is already in the coffin. Plus, don't I have a home here already? What do I need a wife for?'

'*Tiew pathai lhubor* (queen of the night)': Ribor would call Wansuk the flower whose perfume remains even after it has wilted, asking her for money because the younger sister khadduh, who was his official caretaker, was too young to earn and still at school. Wansuk dutifully gave her uncle a share of her earnings from her salary which she earned as a teacher at the evening school. 'My mother will smile upon this act, serving the uncle or the kni.' Wansuk smiled in her thoughts. If the Khasis recognize the youngest daughter (khadduh) of the group as its priestess, then the oldest maternal uncle (kni) was its priest. Protecting and maintaining the well-being of the members of a matrilineal group was the constant activity or role of the maternal uncle. Although an alcoholic, Ribor was supposed to be the spiritual and moral guide for his sisters' children and provide for them if the need arose.

Ancestral property, which was the home they lived in, and some gold, which had been accumulated for two to three or more generations, was held in trust and transmitted from the youngest daughter to her youngest daughter under his supervision and control. And though the youngest daughter had numerous familial and kinship obligations to keep after inheriting the family property, she did not possess the authority commensurate with her duties and responsibilities.

The strain generated by role conflict[24] affected the Khasi women more intensely. A woman could not be fully sure that her husband had more loyalty towards her and her children than towards his sister and her children, to whom he is the kni. Besides, the women secretly felt that their rights and privileges in society turned out to be more burdensome duties and responsibilities; they not only had to manage finances, but also look after the family and children, whereas the role of the father was ambiguous.

\* \* \*

A few years later, while still in college, Syrpai fell in love.

'You're the khadduh.[25] Jimmy has an eye on your property!' bellowed the grandmother from a recently-acquired wheelchair.

Syrpai rolled her eyes. What property, she wondered. A three-bedroom home behind the abode of the rats of Iewduh?

'Do not harbour hate, grandmother. At least Jimmy is a Khasi. And he adores me,' she pleaded.

'He is a Christian! They encourage marriages within the clan. Do you know what a sin it is for a traditional Khasi to marry anyone remotely related to your mother's family?' the grandmother hissed, turning different shades of red.

'But nobody in his family has . . .'

'Wansuk, you have seen him. What kind of a person do you think he is?' the grandmother turned to the older sister.

'I don't think he's any kind of person at all,' Wansuk retorted, continuing with her sewing.

'See, she never says a bad word about him,' Syrpai said.

Not a good word, either.

'I spoke to his aunt. He ran away a day before he was to get married.'

'That's a lie.'

You think a man, any man, would remain a bachelor till he met you, Wansuk murmured, so softly that only she could hear herself; despite her best intent, she had become one of those people who talked to themselves when the world was not paying heed to her judiciousness. When Syrpai announced her final decision to marry Jimmy, she reached for the cigarette packet hidden behind her jainsem; resting her hand lightly on it, assuring herself of its presence.

A week before their wedding, grandmother hosted a *ka-niam-ap*, an expensive feast to honour their dead, revering the memories of deceased ancestors and adoring them by means of offerings. She refused to invite Jimmy.

'He is not a part of the *kur* yet,' grandmother stated, as Syrpai protested. The immediate kur, or clan, of their aunts and uncles from the maternal side were to come; a Khasi has no church, house or temple to worship God, but each and every clan has its own *iingseng iingkhatduh* (the residence of the youngest in the lineage of each clan), where all necessary religious rites and ceremonies are performed. To honour dead ancestors is the only real religious duty and demand of every Khasi, and he who wilfully neglects this duty, it is believed, will neither receive their help, nor be defended from the influence of numerous evil spirits such as pox, diarrhoea and even a smelly backside.

Before the ceremony, Wansuk and Syrpai brought in hot pots of *nakham bitchi*, a fish soup that their uncles loved. The oily broth swirled, the hot spices wafted up and watered their eyes. They laid down bowls of dal with *rumbai*, fermented sesame paste, *tungtap*, and lots of pork. A good Khasi must always serve pork to her guests. The women worked mechanically, serving nuts and pepper, uncorking bottles, shovelling ice as guests poured in: her grandmother's sister came in with her noisy walking stick; the aunts came in later with their children. Ribor and two other uncles of the family, perched high on a plump sofa, happily flooded themselves with homemade rice beer.

The Rynjah family could be clannish. Every Sunday, and on holidays, they gathered in the home of this or that member. Vacations, too, instead of being spent at a lake house or at the shore, were spent visiting one another.

They'd discuss work, weather and extended family, but eventually, one of the aunts would voice the age-old complaint of the Christian Khasis vs the traditional Khasis.

'Christians need saints to talk to God. For us, all we need is mothers and uncles, the priestess and the priest. But the girls today . . .' one of them said while other aunts shook their heads, casting sideways glances at Syrpai, who was cringing in her seat.

'The Christians think they are superior to the indigenous Khasis. Face to face, they are polite, they sell them goods, and sometimes eat at their tables . . . then turn around to bray and snicker about our rituals behind their backs,' Ribor remarked. And so the tension had simmered over the decades, both sides adversarial towards each other. The angst continues, now latent, now effervescent, often flaring into demonstrations and harassment.

'Well, better finish your food. Too much talk only ends in iniquity,' the grandmother intervened.

'Am I not eating? I am eating what you call soup, with specks of fish. What else am I doing? The only thing that's left for me is eating. The truth is that there are no more good women anywhere. Last week, I saw Khasi girls, straight after sermons in the morning, walking down the alleys in skirts. Where are their *dharas*?[26] In my time, there were still some good, dutiful Khasi women . . . but now all they want is a man to be a slave to their needs,' Ribor ranted and glared with red, drunken eyes, waiting for Syrpai to crumple.

Even with the sun at a less-than-satisfactory angle, the grandmother hurried the ritual's start. A little corner was created in the house with offerings of five betelnuts, five bananas, biscuits and rice along with a pot of water around an urn. After offering prayers, they were kept out for the night, should the ancestors visit and like a midnight snack. Through it all, there was humming and chanting; a bit primal. Ribor, more than a bit slurry by then, couldn't act as a priest so another uncle filled in, asking the women of the family to raise their hands. It was kind of chaotic, with the killing of a fowl thrown in: a taste of what the missionaries may have reacted against. In the middle of this all stood an urn.

'In Shillong, people never really die,' grandmother would tell them when they were children.

'But grandmother, people in Shillong are always dying,' Wansuk would argue. 'They die during childbirth, don't they? They die in landslides. Those Burmese soldiers[27] who lived here in Shillong until only a few years ago, they died too: They died from sickness, they died of chagrin, or broken hearts.'

But what Wansuk didn't fully understand was that in Shillong, her grandmother meant, it is the spirit of people that never really dies. Their bones are stored in the urn along with those of their ancestors and kept in the khadduh's house.

'One day, it would house her own bones too,' Wansuk thought to herself, as she carefully cleaned the sacred urn from outside after the last guest left. She walked around the house, straightening the curtains, rearranging the books. She wiped the bone china tea set before carefully putting it back in the cabinet. A cup with a long crack was kept back in, just like saved biscuit boxes, old filled notebooks, ribbons and plastic bags. It came with never having had much as a child, the inability to let go of things, even things that were useless.

Outside, she watered the orchids, sprinkling some sugar for black ants crawling along the hedge. She nudged the mud around the flowers, adding dry wood and coal powder, moving with a painstaking deliberation. This was her favourite part of the day, parenting her collection of orchids, polishing their leaves and trimming their stem; hers was the best pot of orchids all down the road.

'That is cucumber of mice,' she named the smallest of the weeds growing among the orchids to a botanist who came visiting, weeks later. Silver-rimmed glasses, hair parted to one side; he was what Wansuk would call 'clean'. A Niam Khasi by faith, Ronny worked at a lab in the college where she taught; he had borrowed a dried orchid ovary from Wansuk to grow in the lab but it could produce only two tiny leaves; he was there to see Wansuk's collection and take notes.

'Orchids are protected by the roots, not by the seeds,' she told him gently. 'You need to feed them dry wood and coal. How can you grow it in a lab? When you are separating the root from it, you should know when to separate it. Like the baby feeding on the blood of the mother in the womb,' she said, looking up from watering a set of flowers. 'In the wild, orchids grow on trees. But it is not a parasite, stealing its nutrients. It derives nutrients from the tree's surroundings, like bird droppings and decaying leaves.

'Look at this orchid.' She pulled a pot before him. 'An insect was drawn to pollinate it and got stuck there; the flower, thinking it had found its mate, grew around it and into the shape of the insect.'

'Wonderful. And this, what will this look like when it blooms?' Ronny asked Wansuk about a brownish outcrop.

She looked at him with a smile. 'They are already blooming. Some species are plain, you know.'

Long after she had shown him all the orchids, he lingered on, and she could see that there was no reason for him to hurry home. He was born near Cherrapunji, grew up here, studying and now working at a lab in the newly established North Eastern Hill University. He was widowed, and had one teenage son.

There they went again: accumulating people and their burdens along the way. Wansuk could see Ronny's life unfolding before her: he'd work his days in that cold lab till he was too old to be useful, then he'd sit in a wheelchair and curse his life while his son moved on with his family. Wansuk, herself a single, uncommitted woman, felt greater than him and larger than life.

They went out for tea once a week, carefully splitting the bill to the last penny on Wansuk's insistence. One day, due to strikes, the school shut unexpectedly and he insisted they go to Mawphlang[28] where they could spot wild orchids. Oh, Mawphlang! Wansuk always wanted to visit Mawphlang. This prehistoric forest had been preserved by the Lyngdoh clan of the Khasis, the traditional medicine men. It was believed that the deities lived in these groves and for this reason, no one was allowed to take even a dead leaf or pick a flower from this forest, litter it or even utter foul words. The biodiversity of this community-protected forest is impressive, with about 450 species of flora and fauna, attracting rainclouds and keeping the temperatures cool.

For a Khasi, God is present in nature, on the hills, mountains, rivers, lakes, forests, and so Mawphlang was a well-loved reserve. A few miles outside Shillong, the country changed from the window of their city bus: from long pines to rolling, open mist-sprinkled grassland; a rivulet ran into bushes that hid a forest. They walked into a freshly cut dark hole in the bushes that emerged into a forest, with trees rising like giant cathedral columns into the canopy, and a thick carpet of crunchy leaves. A 700-year-old oak trunk was leafless, struck by lightning years ago; no one ventured close to it, a bit overwhelmed by its strangeness in a forest of green. Other trees around it were wreathed in rare white, pink and violet orchids. Jackfruits that had fallen the previous night lay around them, oval and yellow, smelling over-sweet as they rotted; a family of ladybirds leisurely crawled their way up along one of them. A short way off, monoliths were scattered along a slope, used decades ago for cock and bull sacrifices. Droplets of blood, which, when seen closely, were flowers from a rhododendron bush, were scattered around the monoliths. Above, on some rumpled bark, a Wren babbler lifted its beak and whistled. Its mate picked up the strain and repeated it. A crested finchbill watched it all, unperturbed.

'Last week, a couple was caught doing indecent things here,' Ronny said, breaking the reverie Wansuk had slid into. 'The *rangbah-shnong* (head of the durbar[29]) grabbed his collar and threw him out. One elder of the durbar publicly threatened to hang him from a tree.'

Wansuk shook her head in disappointment. Not sure if she had shaken her head in disapproval of the act or the punishment, he hesitantly continued:

'What if they think we are a couple too?'

Could it be that he had agreed to bring her here for a reason other than the orchids they wanted to see?

'Nobody,' she said, walking a little ahead of him, 'will think anything.'

On the drive back, he looked outside and said:

'You should find someone. This is not a good life for you, living in your sister's house.'

'What's wrong with that? I don't pay rent.'

'What's the point of making money from school if you don't spend it?' Ronny retorted. 'At least I'm saving my money for my son and his family.'

'How I use my money,' Wansuk concluded calmly, 'is none of your business.'

Wansuk knew he was well-intentioned, and this talk would only lead to where it often led: of a future together. But men were complicated, and if she were to tell him stories of her family, he'd lose all hope of winning her affection. But where would she start? With her grandfather who drank himself to an early grave, or with the father who didn't even bother knowing if they were alive? Or perhaps she should start with Syrpai's husband, who had vanished last week, only a few months into their marriage. The disappearance would have made sense had Jimmy been a villain, but he was a kind man, clinging to the hope that his wife would one day bestow on him some attention.

Syrpai, a part-time librarian, would take care of their ailing grandmother, while Wansuk struggled with her job at the school and training to be a typewriter. Jimmy had told her he too wanted to take care of her family, live with them forever. He was courting; he was lying; no one hated living in one place more than him; he was always an explorer. Within days of their marriage, he had travelled to Manipur, Nagaland, Kolkata and even as far as Madras to meet friends. She said she couldn't; she had her grandmother and an uncle to tend to. Also, if he was travelling, at least one of them had to work for it. Jimmy's relatives told Syrpai that he was having affairs on his travels, but she loved him with a fierce steadiness borne of loyalty and determination.

'We hardly have any disagreement between us,' she told them. 'It is all peaceful.'

Jimmy remembered it differently. 'I think her family is prone to being a little uptight.'

'I'm scared,' Jimmy said one evening to Syrpai. 'Not of your grandmother or your sister who we live with. I'm scared of this room, your house. These are the kinds of things you have to have known about since childhood. It seems like it's too late for me to learn them.'

'But I cannot move out. I have responsibilities, the people, this house and our sacred urn to take care of. And you're a khadduh's husband.'

He loved no one too long. She loved no one better. He left her for his third cousin, whom he supposedly fell in love with in a romantic French town too far south: Pondicherry.

Waving Ronny off at the gate, Wansuk knew she will never meet Ronny again. Unlike her sister, mother and grandmother, she had talked herself into being a woman with an unremarkable life.

* * *

The sisters, now octogenarians, sit by the window of their ancestral home, watching the world through the frost. Until tonight, Wansuk and Syrpai had never thought about death; they were too busy with the baggage of old age to waste time anticipating the finish line.

They eat their soup as an officer comes knocking on the door.

'Here is it,' Wansuk murmurs.

'We knew it was coming, didn't we?'

A bulb in a lamp on a side table flickers and fizzes.

The officer hands a letter and leaves. Wansuk shouts after him, 'This is our house. Our land! Us, the Khasis. You bastards can't throw us out.'

'The medical facility has to be expanded. Someone has to sacrifice,' the officer mumbles.

'Why can't you expand it where you are building the church . . . sacrifice, you tell me . . .'

What was in the plot opposite their home had been demolished. A pit had been dug and girders and pillars stacked. A church had appeared on the far corner of the plot with a cross so tall and narrow that it looked like it might topple. Syrpai looked at Wansuk huffing as she tottered back in and locked the door behind them. 'Finish that packet of soup.' She snapped at her older sister. 'At the old age home', we will at least get freshly cooked meals.'

In the night, Wansuk could hardly sleep; she sat up in bed and thought of her grandmother; how she was frightened at the thought of being taken away from home. Each time they had taken her to the hospital, thick tears had flowed down her dusty-white skin as she waved a finger at her and Syrpai, 'Can't take care of me at home, you lazy buffoons.'

Around three, Wansuk walked out to the window, still sleepless. She popped a pill as the local gang drove their bikes past their homes, waving their hockey sticks victoriously in the air. Wansuk sat and listened to the roar of their engine and felt certain that she would never be able to come back to this house; that whatever happened, she could never come back.

# 6

# THE KONYAKS OF NAGALAND

*A city-bred Konyak visits his grand-uncle,*
*a former head-hunter*

## Mon district, Nagaland

Pangshong pushes out into the evening air, sucking in great breaths as if starving for it. His head feels like an overstuffed cushion that might quietly implode. That smell, of sweet flowers burning to a char, fogs his mouth, spreads through his shoulders and opens his chest like wings. He would fly if he could, over to the porous Indo-Myanmar border that sprawls before him; landing on an emerald spot of foliage in Loji, Burma's military township. Instead, he lies here on a bare hillock in Longwa, northern Nagaland. Closing his eyes for a few minutes, he tries to keep his lunch down; his thoughts get foggy, packing themselves into neat little boxes. This slow languor, this illusionary bliss, is what his relatives had cautioned him about when he told them of his first visit to Nagaland. When he turns to look back into the room, the *angh* is still at it. He is at it all the time.

The angh, king of Longwa's Konyak tribe, has the longest bamboo home in Longwa, and the only one with a dedicated opium room. A constant fire is maintained in this square den by the angh's aide, a thin and sallow man who mostly sleeps in the room under a thick blanket, even on warm days, and gets up only to prepare opium for the angh or his visitors. Over a heap of glowing embers, lit by shafts of afternoon sunlight coming in through the knotholes in the bamboo walls, the man smears the opium on to a metal spoon along with shaved leaves, holding it over the fire. Poking the bubbling opium into the neck of a carved wooden pipe, or the *chung*, the aide holds a piece of red-hot charcoal to its neck, drawing his few puffs with sips of black tea, before passing it to Pangshong.

The angh of Longwa[1] seldom goes out of the longhouse, apart from a ritualistic, customary Sunday church outing like today, or to shake hands with an illustrious minister or tourist if badgered to do so. In an opium candour, small talk seems dull to a smoker, choirs too perky. He seeks solitude to enjoy the hum. Pangshong tries to persuade him into a conversation about changing times for the Konyak tribe, but the angh has his eyes set on his special deer bone chung. He pulls on it greedily, keeping it in his lungs; his red eyes droop and his body becomes immobile, rapidly yielding to the ecstasy and waiting for the immense euphoria to descend.

If you dug down into the angh's genes, what you'd find at the bottom is a field of poppies. His father was a small man who smoked all his life, his sixty-odd wives taking turns at filling pipes for him. With a lifelong opium smoking career, the current angh, perhaps in his thirties, hardly has the energy to maintain so many spouses. He is happy with two wives, who often visit their mothers in Arunachal while concubines keep him company. The angh has no timepiece that works throughout the house. Or even a real schedule.

Longwa, in the Mon district of Nagaland, has a border that runs right through the middle of the angh's home: the last—and the only successful—attempt by the British to gain control over the fiercely independent Nagas. The border through Naga territory has left them straddling both India and Myanmar, neither of which they feel any kinship or loyalty to. Earlier that morning, the children, holding dual citizenships of both the countries, start walking to the Amaka Lungwa Theinka, a primary school across the border run by the Myanmar government. Their mothers watch them walk with bags hanging on their heads. Most of their fathers are away for work—some soldiers of the Indian army, and some with the Myanmar army.

As the sun sinks behind the hills, Pangshong sees the angh carrying the profound royal lethargy that fills up his bones, across the bodies of his aides and associates sprawled in the opium lair, to stand outside his bamboo hut. He waits for the night man to walk across the unmanned, borderless border of India and Burma on which his imperial home stands. The night man will bring with him the best bag of opium in his basket, crossing the border unchecked, shielded by the dark, into the land of the free, almost self-ruling Konyaks who are protected by Article 371A of the Indian Constitution.[2]

* * *

The mountains sizzle with a certain tamed energy as the taxi swerves around the hills; Pangshong shivers as the gust rakes over the green of the rice fields, and in some secluded stretches, bends the lollipop colours of the opium-rich poppies. There is only one way to reach this part of Nagaland: it has no airports, no trains or buses. A taxi can be tested for hours on the roads that are essentially narrow dust and stone mule paths winding across the lofty mountains that end up in Burma. On either side, hundreds of kilometres of thick, magnificent jungles creep up the steep slopes of the Patkai hills, the range that divides the region from the rest of India. Tall palms and bamboos of the hilly rainforest become silhouettes against the dark clouds that pause behind lofty peaks, pawing at them like bulls.

When the taxi driver stops for a smoke break, Pangshong sits on a rock under the lambent, broken cloud light, his cigarette glowing against a valley of hillocks with a little bamboo hut on each of their tops: a typical Konyak village setup. He may have spent a day in Longwa, but that was just a detour; he was actually here to visit his ancestral hometown farther down near Shangyu. For the years that he grew up in Delhi and then London, he hardly learnt about his Konyak roots or their way of life. His family tree evoked his interest only four years back, at his father's funeral. At the service, he shed no tears as he delivered an eulogy. Later, his uncle walked up to him, patting his back, 'You're a true Konyak *naomei*[3] or warrior.' The lack of tears may have been more to do with the fact that he felt little emotion towards his estranged father, but in any case, later, at the dinner table, his uncle narrated their family's tales, and his Konyak heritage: the blustering swaggering conduct, the bonhomie among the men of the villages, the opium, the human heads they hunted until only a few decades ago, his ancestors' loincloths, long hair and black teeth. It would have been naïve to ignore the differences between him—born in Dimapur and raised in Delhi—and his young uncle, who recently moved from a small Naga village town to Delhi. But the similarities—temperamental, social and imaginative—struck him. They shared an easy conversation: He was not shocked that his uncle too loved snake soup, was fiercely independent and detested control. However much Pangshong's parents loathed, and denied, their Konyak heritage, they couldn't help retain personality traits, preserved by inheritance, and, in turn, pass them on to him. That evening, after the funeral, Pangshong knew he wanted more of the sense of family, the past and the people out of that past.

In the car, every once in a while, Pangshong sees a lone Naga man or woman walking down the hills with a basket on their back with produce from their fields or forests, and machetes. Almost everyone has a rudimentary gun. Despite the long stretches of jungle, animals in these hills are rarely visible. He comes across one lone *mithun* on the two-hour drive to the village; seeing the car, it gallops back into the forest. Elephants are almost extinct here. Monkeys that casually hang on the road rails in hills across India prefer the treetops here in dense thickets instead. They seem to fear the Konyaks, a Naga tribe whose homes lie here and there, in the shadows of the forest, lost in time.

Dark clouds start gathering as Pangshong approaches his hometown, Sheanghag Chingnyu, in Mon district.

The taxi rattles on the terrible roads. As they close in on his village, it starts raining—thick sheets of rain, as if kids were hiding behind the bushes and hurling water at him. Enormous trees along the hills stretch their gnarled branches against the sky; the impenetrable undergrowth makes it tough to walk. Yet, on the top of hills, open to all storms, the bamboo houses cling to the rocks. He waits for the rain to stop before climbing out of the car. Four or five children peek out of the hut: the plum-cheeked, sunburnt faces of hill boys and girls.

'Wangloi Wangshu's home?' he asks the kids.

One of them puts one hand on his waist and puts out the other.

Others giggle, perhaps at Pangshong's clean white sneakers or his accent.

Unsure, Pangshong hands him his half-eaten bar of chocolate. Shaking his head, the boy gives it to his friend who distributes the pieces among the others. When Pangshong opens his wallet, they get excited looking at the new Indian currency notes after the demonetization of 2016.[4] It's been a few months and in the absence of ATMs, the notes are yet to reach this neck of the woods. It is only when a new note has been held against the sky and checked for authenticity that Pangshong is led to his ancestral home.

They cross a longhouse, known as the *morung* or boys' dormitory that his uncle had told him about: 'It was a bachelor house of sorts for the boys where they trained for wars and prepared for village festivals, hunting expeditions and other social engagements.' It is mostly empty now except for a massive fifteen-foot log drum used to make announcements. There is a semblance of a plan in their arrangement, with the morung that dominates the entrance to the village and good-sized bamboo shanties hanging on ridges or on spurs. Up in the hills, the Nagas have busy lives: While grandparents and older siblings take care of babies, most adults go to the fields, with a community-based approach to farming. A group of people move from field to field; they hardly snack and have time for only two meals a day and a few rounds of opium. Most men and women are probably taking shelter from the rain in the granaries of the fields they work in, while the elderly are managing the children and homes. Climbing another hillock, Pangshong reaches his grand-uncle Wangloi Wangshu's home. A family of pigs rootles gloomily in the bare earth, a rooster crows, there is some sort of pounding from the hut and a woman tells a cat off: sounds that form a village. There are many emotions that Pangshong's heart and mind are brimming with, but he is not yet able to comprehend them. His father, who was born in this house, never missed it, he'd insist. Mostly, he hated it.

A single source of light, the door, admits the sun's rays into the windowless bamboo hut, and on to the central hearth of firewood. There is a rack just above the central kitchen fire, and pork, chicken, taro and tapioca hang from it to be smoked and preserved for the colder days.

Pangshong's grandaunt, Ayong, in her late eighties, dressed in a skirt and sweater, chirps and flits around the house like a wren babbler, slicing a papaya for him, adding dried black tea leaves from her bush to a tin kettle while remembering his father: 'Oh, whenever that boy came with his father to our village, he devoured the dried pork but hated sleeping on the mats. That city-bred lad was afraid of snakes,' she cackles.

Wangloi, his grand-uncle, wearing shorts and a 'cowboy' T-shirt, squints at him. He first looks at him as if he is a threat, but as Pangshong sits closer to him, he takes in his cleft chin, pointed ears and the crinkly eyes; those can only belong to a Wangshu, he mutters with a half-smile.

Pouring a small amount of black tea into each glass, he offers one to him. It is a Konyak welcome offering of sorts, indicating that he is welcome to stay awhile. Pangshong looks around his two-room ancestral house where his grandfather grew up; a constant ruddy fire in both rooms to keep the caterpillars and moss away and the room warm. The sharp edges of a machete, *dao*, or axe, and two guns hanging on the bamboo walls shine in the darkness of the hut. A small Jesus figurine lies on a shelf along with a packed copy of the Bible. In the last few years, his grand-uncle's family have given in to the pressure of going to the church in the nearby village, if not completely converting to Christianity.

Alongside are heads of bull, bear, deer and rats. 'I hunted most of them,' Wangloi grunts when he catches him staring at the skulls. 'A few were taken by your father's father too. He left for Kohima in the sixties and I never met my milksop brother again.'

Follower of the indigenous animist religion, Pangshong's own grandfather had surgically removed his Konyak face tattoos in Kohima, married a devout Christian, and refused to ponder over their 'uncivilized' past or tell his children or grandchildren about his days spent in this village as a child. Pangshong's father too had a tendency to think in stark terms: traditional tribals had black teeth, hunted for a pastime and ate raw meat, while the converted Christian Nagas were 'civilized'. He made sure he excelled in school, and, feeling confined by the Nagamese,[5] made a point of becoming skilled at 'proper' English. Like his father, he married a Naga Christian who dressed up for church every Sunday, said nightly prayers and would 'raise the children right'. On moving to Delhi with his wife and children, his father insisted on picking up Hindi, and found it comforting to have access to a language that his family back in Kohima could not comprehend. 'We are Christians,' his father snapped, while his mother closed her eyes and said a quick prayer for his sanity, when once Pangshong asked him about their Konyak heritage. 'Nothing else.'

'The skin on those heads was removed,' Wangloi breaks into his thoughts. 'The heads were boiled before hanging them up here. We used to do the same with human heads,' Wangloi continues with what Pangshong suspects is pride. 'Now, the human heads lie covered in a ditch down that hill.'

Wangloi has black teeth and cheeks lined with tattoo ink. Only animals have white teeth, the Konyaks believed until a few years ago. When he laughs, he seems aggressive, though he does not mean harm. His eyes are calm, movements measured, but he has this way of speaking—as if he prefers demonstrating his love and anger more than talking about it. When he manages to grate some words out, it is more like a sound—a roar or grunt or bark. He is just slightly feral, Pangshong thinks, dismissing his concern.

When Wangloi was enrolled in the morung back in the day, which was sort of a school-cum-community centre where all the boys from the tribe were registered, his foremost education, he says, would be in 'virility',[6] which Pangshong's father thought was a disgusting word, full of sexual connotations and misogyny. His father preferred the less offensive and somewhat dull word 'masculinity'. For his ancestors, meanwhile, virility was the foremost feature of exemplary men. Virile men win it all: wars, women and big game hunting. At the morung, they learnt and observed other boys and men, and sought to ally virility with violence. They also learnt to fight without getting angry, or to make themselves heard without shouting.

'My grandfather used to say, "Eat with a spear in the hand. The enemy won't wait for you to finish eating".' Wangloi laughs, baring his teeth again. 'A "good naomei" protected his comrades and never refused a beautiful woman's advances. Our village must grow bigger, stronger and for that, enemies' heads must be secured, brought to the village and fed rice beer. This would bring it prosperity and for the naomei, some virility. The more the heads, the more the reverence.'

As a baby, Wangloi was big despite his Naga genetics, which should have caused him to be small. He conspicuously crawled about in the morung as his grandfather sharpened his spears or mended hunting nets, while younger men manned the village outposts and bunkers. The morungs had no real head of the organization, but the valorous and the experienced often took the lead. Meetings were held among the villagers about the allocation of duties so that all villagers were mutually obligated to help each other in head-hunting wars, in the fields, for building or rebuilding houses and during festivals, marriages and other social occasions.

At the morung, Wangloi was always a bit of an odd fish, but he was the last kid anybody in the village expected to take heads. Not a droller, a brave heart or a joker, he was not widely held in high regard. Of course, there was his nonchalance—his feathers remained unruffled even when given the most complicated of tasks. Still, Wangloi used to make such a song and dance about his composure that you'd have thought he was the gentlest of them all.

Young children were accompanied everywhere within and around the village by the parents or grandparents for the fear they would be killed by animals or head-hunters. But after a few months in the morung, Wangloi could fraternize with the boys from the morung, working in the fields, killing game and practising war skills. The older boys in the morung taught him to build bunkers, extract poison from 'faraway' trees to make arrows and most important of them all—to hate their enemies and to prepare themselves for a life of fighting as a naomei, a warrior.

Late into his adolescence, Wangloi was finally initiated as a naomei into the morung along with his peers, with a big ceremony involving a pig's sacrifice and a song:

*'Hi, hi, hi, ha, ha, ha, yu my shi mei enek mu shi mei kheang phe'*

Roughly translated, the song means 'May my rice beer increase, may my rice become plentiful, may all enemies, all head-takers and all anghs eat from my rice.' They then drank copious amounts of rice beer, danced around posts that were elaborately carved with elephants, hornbills and tiger and a peculiarly elongated image: a penis in a state of erection.

It is hard to say where the Konyak Nagas come from: their head-hunting traditions are similar to the Dayaks of Malaysia[7] while their language is Sino-Tibetan. The Nagas seem to have no written historical record about their origin and the route of migration to their present habitation. Some writers believe that the Nagas immigrated from three directions: north-east, north-west and south-east.

In the absence of a script, verbal records passed from generation to generation narrate that the ancestors of most Konyaks came from a peak called Yengyudang. Another, and equally widespread, folk tale tells of a migration from mainland China via the Brahmaputra valley along the Dikhu River and into the hills flanking that river.[8] However, it is a general belief that the majority of the Nagas immigrated from the south-east through the corridor of the Indo-Myanmar border to the Naga Hills. So fierce was their competition for territory and resources that they were enemies with most of their immediate neighbours. They produced sophisticated weapons like bombs and guns in their homes, making themselves practically, and geographically, impossible to defeat. Their neighbours in Assam and Burma, and later the British, were wary of their fierce guerrilla warfare: an intimidating mosaic of animism, totemism, magic, of sacred fire and gold, of reverence for sun, moon, sky, earth, nature, wild animals and fantastic creatures.

As the evening approaches, Pangshong shifts his stool closer to the fire. Wangloi bends to shift the cinders and stoke the fire. A dust cloud rises and smokes the air in front of him with fine grit; he squints against it. His profile becomes prominent in the leaping fire: the wrinkled, tattooed face brushed with raw gold, his cloudy eyes, bent knees, the shrivelling body of a ninety-year-old man. Along with his facial wrinkles were souvenirs of his successful head-hunt: long grey lines of tattoo made by the queen, or their village angh's wife, on each of his victorious returns with the heads.

'I was fifteen, or sixteen, when I first took a head,' Wangloi narrates. It is strange, Pangshong reflects, that his black teeth and timbre, which should arouse suspicion, elicit sympathy instead. 'The fire that night had just died when the hollow drum in the morung sounded *gon-gon-gob*. I ran out wondering what was wrong,' for the drum going off in the night certainly meant something was wrong. His aunt was already sitting outside the hut alongside his, cradling her worrying bosom in her arms while her son was

by her side, pressing his face into her. Her young daughter
had not returned from the fields that day; the older men
in the morung had gone out with search parties. The
hearth was lit again as they sat waiting, a gang of moths
flapping hopelessly around it. Suddenly, there were cries
and screams of men and women as the drums sounded off
and soon after came the news brought by the search party:
'Our beloved cousin was killed while working in the fields;
her head hunted by warriors of a neighbouring enemy
village. They had taken her head and left the body.' Tears
had sprung to his eyes then, but he refused to let them fall.
What if a morung boy saw it?

In the hills where Wangloi and his clan lived, his cousin
had played a big role in raising him. For years, he did not
even distinguish between his biological mother, who was
always tending to the rice, and this cousin sister; her death
demanded revenge.

'That night, I could feel anger rise from the tips of my
toes and burst into my head. I wanted to tear someone
apart with my bare hands,' he whispers looking coolly into
Pangshong's eyes; none of the anger he talks about reflects
on his face, desensitized perhaps after seeing years of deaths.
His cousin's dead body was left on a tree, headless, while
the hornbills watched over it. When it would decompose
after several days, parts of it would be kept in a specially
designed sandstone urn through which the family members
could provide food to the dead person.

The next morning, villagers gathered outside the
morung. There was the angh, a wimpy man, with a queen

sitting on a pedestal; men and women standing before him murmured about last night's occurrences. Villages around Mokukchung were converting through missionaries' pleas for peace-keeping, but here in Mon, head-hunting was nowhere close to its end yet. At last, Wangloi had stood up before the angh: 'How dare they kill my sister?' he questioned the angh, meekly at first. 'How dare they kill my sister?' he shouted this time, his face reddened with restrained anger. One after the other, men rose and screamed too, 'Revenge. We demand revenge.'

Each naomei, or a warrior, around here lugged around a long roster of dead mates, wives or children, parents, lovers, siblings, clan members, blacksmiths or even a childhood playmate. 'Every year, we lost hundreds of such villagers, so hating the enemy came naturally to us. And it came early . . .' Wangloi falters, thinking his own burdensome thoughts. It's no wonder that he, and many other warriors in the village like him, were a bit bent, working against gravity, so that the accumulated weight of these departures didn't bury them.

'If you fight when that feeling of anger is on top of your mind, you'll expose yourself, and it will be easy for the enemy to kill you,' an older boy at the morung had told Wangloi as they had made a long two-day journey to the enemy village. A group ten to twelve strong, brave, young men, would first attack a village. If they sounded for help, others waiting in the dugouts outside would join them.

The Konyaks were expert warriors; they were extremely territorial and allowed no strangers to enter their lands.

Besides revenge, there were ongoing border disputes and open war challenges. But attacking a Konyak village was no mean task; steep slopes and heavy rainfall made the streams swell. Even for the mainland people, frequent head-hunting wars made journeys between villages difficult.

The British, meanwhile, first came into contact with the Nagas in 1832, when Captain Jenkins and Pamberton, along with 700 soldiers and 800 coolies, marched across the Naga Hills in their attempt to find a route from Manipur to Assam. Fighting for heads, and defending their villages, the Nagas would attack the British. Eventually, it flared up into a war that continued until the 1880s, when the fort of Khonoma finally fell into the hand of British troops. The British gained control over many Naga territories, but the Konyak Nagas were never defeated. After multiple ambushes in the 1800s, the British gave up, stationing themselves lower in the hills and planting opium close to the Konyaks, hoping, in vain, to numb their savagery. They were successful to a certain extent when a large number of anghs gained access to an overwhelming amount of opium, which slowly gained popularity among the commoners too, and along with rice beer, made them some of the most rapid converts to Christianity.

Before that, the Konyaks still had no broad tribal identities. Every morung was a nation unto itself, every hilltop a democracy, and these war-hungry Nagas[9] raided the British troops from different villages; cheap heads of defenceless warriors were only too welcome. In case of retaliation from the British, they posted sentinels around

villages, up to ten kilometres from their village, in order to
protect their homes, fields and sheep pens. The forests were
lined with spiked bamboo traps called *panjers* that could
pierce the feet; there were strings that released poisoned
arrows straight into the victim's ribs. It is said that a certain
British officer once lost three of his troops when they fell
into a concealed pit full of large spears.

An almost perpetual mist that lay in these hills made
it easier for the Konyaks to move, camouflaging their
movements. Sometimes the fog was so thick, they could
not see the enemy village and followed a trail instead. They
moved in single file, up and down the valleys with stones
rolling at their heels; grey clouds crowding in; revenge
pressing them on.

In the nights, they slept under large rocks with spears
by their side. Their wives or mothers would wrap rice
in banana leaves, to be cooked inside holes covered with
charcoal embers to avoid smoke that could warn the
enemies; sometimes they'd just eat preserved smoked
meat or sniff out spots that produced well-developed
taro. Besides, they caught and hunted daily whatever they
could see: monkey heads, cat tails and yak belly. 'Surviving
hunger helped us reach whatever was available . . .'

Pangshong smiles when he hears that. On his travel for
work across South East Asia, he has eaten several things:
grilled pigeon, snake soup, charred dog meat. Clearly, his
genes retained some of his ancestral food habits.

Wangloi is showing him larvae that would be cooked
for dinner when he hears a shout from some young boys

playing war outside their home. The clouds had broken and the sun was out. A group of children, about six or seven years old, held mock guns made from bamboo. The sleekest gun belonged to the tallest child with firm, deep set eyes. 'Teee dededee . . .!' he shouts. It is the Naga sound for victory. And the boys attack with bamboo guns and rush towards the other boys, the neighbouring village's losers. A boy from that team sits on his knees, while the tallest boy pretends to knock him down and then breaks into a dance, hopping like a bird from foot to foot.

Violence is forbidden among the Konyak Nagas these days. The church condemns any talk of war and the past, making it a taboo. They tell them that the new religion is a rebirth, and nothing of the old ways should remain with a person who is born again. Watching the boys play, Wangloi could not say what he was really thinking: 'This was what boys did with other boys.' It was the usual way in these hills for toughening oneself for the future.

But he did say, 'C'mon now, boys, make less noise.'

He smiles with glee nevertheless, exposing his crooked teeth. His wife finally shoos the children away and takes to pounding her rice with more determination. In the fights back then, both sides cooed war songs as they approached the enemy. They sang, 'We killed your brother, and he was a coward,' which stirred their resolve to take life: man, woman or even a child.

'What happened then? Did you get your revenge?' Pangshong asks. Wangloi looks at him, unsure if he should proceed.

'In the enemy village, I found my first victim hiding behind a bush just outside the village,' Wangloi mutters, standing at the door as he looks out at the boys now playing with marbles. 'Eyes wide as a buffalo: a young, unarmed boy. He was the same age as these children.' Wangloi had wanted to sing a war song then as he had lifted his dao, but his voice cracked. But he had mouthed it anyway as he cut the victim's shirt, making long incisions in the jugular vein so that the blood spurted. 'At the sight of blood, my fellow men gave a great shout of victory. I had finally put flowers on my cousin's grave.'

'It didn't matter who it was; what mattered was the head: The hair was held in the hands and the head sliced off. If we caught them alive, we'd hang them up on trees. Once the heads were secured, we'd untie the body from the tree and hurl it into the gloomy ravines.' For a skull that held so much value, it was surprising the body was equally irrelevant. Hyenas would slowly creep to the body, hoping, not without reason, for pickings of the soft viscera, or an enormous gall bladder.

The fighting went on till one of the morung gangs sounded the gong, a low, deep, echoing sound of mourning. Ivory was offered as a sign of surrender and the other side's tools of war were confiscated: helmets made of bear skin, bows and arrows. Despite the Konyaks living in what resembled the Stone Age, often, the war tools also comprised of rudimentary guns.

Early wars were fought with expertly made spears, bows and arrows, and daos, which, with a single movement, could cut down the head of the enemy. But the constant pursuit to better warfare led to guns. Nagas like to claim they were the first ones to make guns, which perhaps marked a watershed in their moral decline; wars turned more savage and bitter. It was a rudimentary gun, with a barrel and trigger made from iron extracted from the riverside. Ten or twelve could be manufactured with iron collected in a year. 'For the bullets, we collected the soil from urinary rooms. That thing is a quite a bomb,' he cackled at his own joke, upsetting a pet cat which makes a dash for the door. 'When you cook that water, and dry it, it becomes powdery, like salt and sugar, and put that in a bullet, it can seriously injure the bravest.'

Most of these wars started ostensibly for skulls. Anthropologists later debated whether the wars in the later years were really for a deeper underlying cause, such as land procurement or food. Politically, head-hunting is believed to be significant because in such raids, the defeated villages become the subjects of the victorious village and therefore have to pay tributes, which they called *poon*. But the warriors themselves, when asked to name a cause of war, usually pointed to the skull. The skulls, according to animism, would bring them prosperity, virility and fertility of soil. The highlanders, for whom cultivation is a lot of hard work in the mountains, are chronically starved for food, which the skull would ensure plenty of.

A day after the war, the queen, the angh's wife, administered the tattoos.[10] The queen of their village lives across from Wangloi's hut, with porcupine ear piercings

and more beads around her neck than her Longwa
counterpart. Taught the craft by her mother, she first
practised it on other women's legs, then their chests.
While the men were away at war, women would go to
jungles to find the *Toona ciliata* tree and make a dent in
its trunk, collecting the oozing sap and then cooking it to
a char. Warriors typically received their tattoos just days
after a successful kill. Mostly, everyone who went to war
deserved to be tattooed, and those who assisted with the
killing or performed heroic deeds during the war got a few
extra lines on their face.[11] When these men would sleep,
their soul would travel into a wild animal, like a leopard.
Through it, they would be able to track the movements of
their enemies. Men who possessed these spiritual assistants
would become leopard-like in their actions and rarely
be defeated in a battle. For the men, the tattoos defined
their rites of passage from boyhood to manhood, and their
achievements in battle. For the woman, it defined her cycle
of life, of having passed from one stage of life to the other.[12]
Often, it took her more than two weeks to complete all the
tattoos of the warriors in her midst. But before the female
tattooist performed the operation, she had to ensure there
were no evil wandering spirits.

Upon hearing about Wangloi and the other warriors'
victory, the tattooist had called upon a shaman, who spoke
to the spirits with a banana leaf wrapped around his finger.
Long after the shaman left, they discovered the spirit had
not gone back: It screeched, echoed along the valley, blew
up their roof and threw a cat over the hill. The angh, or king

of the Sheanghag Chingnyu, who was alive then, bandaged his head in a fox hide to soften the sound, fastening the shrivelled paws beneath his jawbone. With most warriors still not home, he was afraid for his life. 'It was gone by the time we approached the climb to the village.' Wangloi laughs. The windy ghost must have seen them arrive with skulls, dripping with blood.

Killing was like a graduation ceremony. With the trophies of bloody heads in his basket, his revenge won, Wangloi returned with the men and made the first trip to the angh's home, bowing before his chair. With the windy ghost departing earlier that morning, the angh was back on his throne; the return of his village warriors and a dose of opium sedating him in his place. A great deal of rice alcohol was drunk to celebrate the gallant soldiers and dancing went on long into the night. Womenfolk watched them, ready with the festive feast of the best meat; dressed in beads covering their naked breasts and an apron covering their middle (deeper into the hills, people back then still preferred complete nudity, hardly bothered by the cold wind sweeping down their backs). Log drums, that day, were beaten for hours in the morung, the women sometimes taking turns on them if men were too drunk.

'We don't have much music, just a few drums or the buffalo horn. But that was enough to make us dance all night,' Wangloi recalls. 'We'd recount the war to villagers, embellish it with exaggeration. Back then, the more devilish the act, the better it was.'

Wangloi had taken three heads of the nine that were brought back and the villagers, especially women, graced him with admiring respect and lust. They waited with bamboo pipes full of water to wash off the enemy's blood, stroking their chests longer than required, seducing the brave warriors to dark corners. Despite being married, Wangloi bedded young girls, sometimes married, a nice break from his subservient wife. Some bonds were more complicated, like that between him and his male mates at the morung. There was a specific boy who followed Wangloi everywhere he went, hunted, cooked and sharpened his spears, and often, they say, he was the only one who understood his war scars, literally and figuratively—and for a while, their relationship became far more complex, a rule-breaking love affair.

The next day, the morung boys cleaned the head after the elders cracked an egg on it, and then carefully avoiding the lower jaw, which held the spirit of the body, they stripped it down to the skull. The bits of flesh, discarded, were finished by dark, bristly pigs waiting in the shadows.

'They could smell death as they cleaned the blood; and examined the blood-smeared skulls with flies feasting upon them. The thick, dirty smell of rotting flesh wafted through the air, and the children played with the warrior headgear like toys—no one was really disturbed by the carnage.

'It was animals killing each other. What could be disturbing about that?' muttered his grandaunt, continuing her grinding. Pangshong shivers despite the fire warming his hands and toes. When he had asked his grand-uncle about the days of headhunting, he had expected some war stories, not ruthless barbarity.

Outside Wangloi's home, it is getting dark already. The weather conditions around here change swiftly: the sky seems like a theatre with arc lights and curtains. *Now sun! Now rain!* A swelling cloud creeps up on to the hills and the hut turns chilly, cold from currents of air and conversations.

Ayong finishes her grinding and heaves the firewood to the coals, turning the cinder into a roaring fire to warm the house; its sparks flutter up with their truths, hovering till they are cooled off by the mist.

Wangloi says nothing for a while, rubbing his forehead, chafing away his thoughts. A pig outside gets restless and growls. Wangloi walks out—his gait unsteady due to his half-bowed knees—and throws some papaya peels into the sty, muttering something that only the pigs can hear.

His wife stares after him; both of them are strained from the effort of pulling the strands of history that they'd rather bury, just like the skulls. Talking about the brutality of those days seems to make it more real, building on the guilt that the church so eagerly induces in them. It is rare for the church-going Konyaks to speak about their head-hunting days, a practice forbidden by the minister and the village councils at large.

The fire burns and tosses ruddy chunks of light; minutes tick by as the sticks in the fire settle into coals. Ayong had never gone head-hunting, no women in the tribe did. Hunting, fishing and community work like making and repairing homes were a man's job. While her father, brother, husband and cousins went to war, she would fan the embers, smoke meats, blow out the husks in rice after pounding it, pick weevils from beans, and take care of the children, fowl, goats and chickens. If she was graceful, she could also be provocative, exercising moral pressure on her husband, who'd otherwise fish or smoke opium, to go for wars. Her husband's prowess in war would, in turn, promote her own position in the society—she would be a brave heart's wife.

Ayong knew all about Wangloi's women, who indulged his sexual appetite and megalomania that stuck on as inertia after each head-hunting expedition, but days later, when the euphoria died down, he would recede into the dark; he wouldn't talk and couldn't make love for weeks later. Ayong would help him bury the horror of breaking down because he was supposed to put on a good front, no matter how bad his troubles. Behind their bamboo hut doors, she would coax him back to sanity and their mattresses with a little help from opium.

Inside the hut, Wangloi pulls out a bag out of his pocket, undoes the elastic band and tucks a quid of green into his cheek: betel leaf with lime. This is a departure from his opium-smoking habit. The opium habit was a departure from his head-hunting days.

Does he regret the kills? 'No,' he says, spitting red betel juice into a bucket lined with plastic. After a long pause, he adds, 'It wasn't a good way of life but seeing a head was always a mixture of elation and desire.'

On other occasions, he has admitted to his wife about having nightmares '. . . about this young wide-eyed boy hiding behind a bush,' Ayong whispers, feeling the familiar rush of shame that the church insists she feels. It starts in her bosom, hidden beneath the sweater, and rushes on to her cheeks—the heat of it makes her giddy and she grabs a tool and sits on it. In times of war, foes are turned eagerly into figures of hatred, only to stop the hating again as soon as a peace treaty is signed. This leaves the soldiers who fight these wars having a hard time readjusting, feeling emotionally numb and disconnected. When they look back, far from boasting about killings, most Konyak Nagas have nightmares and hardly talk about it.

'The last war,' Wangloi continues, 'was with this village near Shangyu.' His voice seems to be dying somewhere within him; from a roar, it has reduced to a tired rasp as he retires into the mattress. 'In my father's time, we did not fight with this village. Sometime in the early fifties, a man from our village had gone fishing. Shangyu warriors crept up on him and crashed his skull, mistaking him for a warrior from another neighbouring enemy village. They took the head and hid it in the basket—a mistake, because they acquired a whole new set of enemies.'

At ninety, he recounts this seventy-year-old story to Pangshong in an emotionally flat, distant, storytelling way, as if he no longer wishes to attach feelings to the story. It's a tightly controlled act, a way of preserving his sanity while living with his memories.

'Usually, a morung tries to obtain revenge within weeks of a killing while the situation is still tense, and people feel especially aggressive. But that fight was delayed.' The Indian ban against head-hunting was another decade away but the church had already started affecting the morals of the Konyaks.

'A girl from that village was married into Shangyu village and she sent smoke signals to warn her natal relatives about the positioning of their warriors. The warriors surrounded Shangyu, killed about ten people and caught two alive. Of course, it didn't end there. Revenge saw another two women from our village killed in the wee hours of the morning.

'. . . It had to stop somewhere,' he says dismissively. With more access to British-made guns, stronger and better-developed weapons, the primeval head-hunting expeditions were turning into massacres; entire villages were burnt down in some ambushes, killing hundreds. 'Women couldn't walk to the fields alone and children were mostly restricted to the homes; there were too many widows, sometimes many in the same family.'

Around the years after Independence, Mon villages started exchanging their first daos as a peace agreement[13] after some prodding from the evangelists; Christianity filled the void left by the fall of anachronistic traditions. The Konyak Nagas were also the last ones to take up Christianity in this region. They were enticed by the usual trappings—education, medicine and a religion that adopted harmony—even as missionaries sought to abolish their traditions. The church condemned not only the killings; but also encouraged burials instead of leaving

the dead bodies hanging on trees; it shamed nudity and
polygamy. It took a long time; by the turn of the century,
only a handful practised animism and first-generation
learners were at school. They cut their hair short, wearing
leather jackets instead of leaves, and would rather forget
their loutish past, wishing no association with it, except
with rice beer and opium.

'You *waksa*. What are you doing outside?' His grand-
uncle breaks into his thoughts as Pangshong smokes his
cigarette at the edge of the hillock.

'I came out for some fresh air . . .'

'And get torn apart by a wild cat? I don't want that
bastard of a grandfather of yours to curse me from the
skies. Come back in.'

The nights here, he is told, are dangerous. They hold
a particular terror for the Konyaks, even so many decades
after the end of head-hunting. Children and women are
rushed in as soon as the night sets in; even the bravest men,
who kill leopards with one hand, sit by the kitchen hearth
and whisper their conversations. Their homes, Pangshong
observes as he looks around the hut, are still dark with
corners to hide in, no windows, and a constant fire.

Over the turn of the century, the Nagas have shed
their traditions like snakeskin, trading animist ceremonies
for Christian atonements, colourful weaves for T-shirts
and shorts, and folk songs for carols. But at heart, the
Konyak men still desire to be archetypal heroes: tough,
strong, courageous. Back in the day, head-hunters proudly
displayed the human heads they'd collected. Since Jesus

came to town, they still display heads but only animal heads, however sordidly acquired.

Hunting—legalities sorted and conservation issues notwithstanding—still excites the Naga men for the auspicious heads, the meat and for the bravado. The government of Nagaland ratified the Wildlife Protection Act in 1981; the Act makes hunting and killing any protected animal a crime, but most village councils and Nagas assume they are protected by the special provisions of Article 371(A), which states that 'no act of Parliament with respect to religious or social practices of the Nagas, Naga customary law and procedure' etc. shall apply to the state unless the Legislative Assembly decides so by a resolution.

\* \* \*

In the next few days, Pangshong would explore the forests nearby with his cousin, Wangloi's own grandson. One morning, he accompanies him and a small party of six men down to the rainforest. Under the bramble and broken forest, it is dark and stagnant, thunderstorms playing hide and seek in a nearby valley. The men move in groups, outfitted with knives, daos and guns made by the village smith, which, again, need no licence from the Indian government in this part of the world.

The green Sung runs as fast as ever, bubbling at every rock and pool. At a curve of the Sung river, where the animals often come for a drink, the hunters set a snare and a trap line for a deer—its guts were needed for the angh's feast—and spend the better part of the afternoon snacking on the gooseberries. Every now and then, they hear a rustling but the animals are sparse; most of them already hanging as skulls on the walls of Konyak villages around them. When it is time for lunch, the men Pangshong accompanies stoke the fire, make a small drain connecting to the river, where the rushing water collects, bringing along with it a delicious small fish or *nyah*. The fish is served into their palms and mixed with bamboo shoots for a quick meal.

While scooping icy water into his hand for a drink, Pangshong hears the river muttering, making a distant train sound a long way off, but nothing appears on the horizon. After hours of wait, the disappointed party is back on their way back to the village when they suddenly hear some lumbering and cracking of sticks.

In the next three hours, they manage to pull up the black yak uphill. '*Lomi lomi*,' shouts one of the hunters, hurrying the others in case the rope gives away. Outside the village, the yak is tied through its nose to a bunch of bamboo shoots. The hunters had shot a small bullet through its belly, the poison enough to cause pain and its breath to come in sonorous gasps. Yet, it manages to call feebly out to them, drumming its legs on the packed earth floor, fat hooves wildly pattering for an escape.

The elders of the village pour in—men in shorts with tattooed faces, antelope horns pierced through ears, thin hair tied and held together by porcupine needles.

'The yak is to be fed,' declares the chief of the village council, 'until a wedding comes up, when it will be killed and its meat distributed among the family members of the hunters, their neighbours, members of the council; the best piece, the tenderloin, is to be offered to the angh.' The hunters obediently nod along as the unearthly caterwauls of the yak begin. The men head to the chief's home, lounging after a long morning with many rounds of opium and black tea.

Wangloi's grandson, in his late twenties, like Pangshong, bare-chested and in shorts, begins to tell, truthfully or not, the reciprocal nature of the hunt's dangers: 'I fought him, and he and I were locked in a struggle' sorts of tales. If he were not a Naga, Pangshong would not have believed his story: He was a small man, unlike his grandfather, with a tough, dry body that seemed more like that of prey than of a hunter. He tells him stories of wrestling wild dogs, chasing a leopard down the hill and killing two birds with a single shot. 'Once,' he narrated deliberately slowly, highlighting the little details, 'I waited for game by the river, having had a lunch of a bush bird that I shot down from a deodar tree with a slingshot. Five minutes later, a bear surprised me on the rolling logs coming down the river, crystalline drops glistening on his black coat. I rummaged for a gun in my basket, shot the bear with a couple of shots that hit its hind leg and it fell into the river. On the next shot, I realized I had no bullets left; the startled bear was already swimming towards me. But as soon as it came to the bank, it galloped with a lumpish gait and fell down . . .'

'What did you do with the bear? Eat it?' Pangshong asks.

Taking a deep drag of opium, he replies, 'Its head, for our ceremonial head dress. Its fur, for a warm coat. The paw, as a fly swatter.'

Later in the night, Pangshong lies on the rock outside his ancestral hut and closes his eyes. He finally understands where his father's antipathy for the land came from; but deep down, he could never get rid of his pride, his strong sense of independence and his love for larvae soup. As a pre-teen, he had wanted a toy gun to play with his friends. His parents had taken him to the church next day, the priest gave him a sermon, but he finally stole a toy gun from his friend. Tonight, he feels like he is something that just lies under the night skies, like the hillocks outside, and nothing more. He does not want to be anything more but be a part of this land for a while. Perhaps this is what one feels like when they die and become a part of something bigger, something more wholesome.

# NOTES

## Chapter 1: The Halakkis of Ankola

1. Start her menstruation cycle.
2. Traditional songs are a big part of life in the Halakki tribe. There is a song for every occasion, and elderly Halakki men and women pass these songs on to the younger generation as part of the 'oral tradition', which continues through centuries and many generations. Everyday work, festivals, auspicious occasions, cultural events and times when people gather to express emotions—there is a song for every occasion and vice versa.
3. Due to the unavailability of a literal translation for some songs, the closest meanings of most songs in this chapter has been added.
4. A group of Halakki homes.
5. This is a significant practice across south India and is referred to as '*veelya*'.
6. A sort of Hindu mandap for the wedding ceremony.

7. The designs are mostly aesthetic. *Halli* or *seedi* is a popular form of decorating walls and employed during most festive and ritual occasions.

8. Nadavas, or Nadavaru, are known as 'Gaonkars', according to the Halakkis. Halakkis participate in Nadavas's special occasions as porters, doing small chores assigned to them. They work in their fields and homes as labourers.

9. Fishermen would prepare country liquor using jaggery, and, often, certain fertilizers would be added to increase the potency.

10. The drape around the neck, leaving the back bare, is known by the Halakkis as the *gitaki* style.

11. Silver necklace worn by married women.

12. Halakkis celebrate the harvest festival in which Suggi Mela (drum beaters) wear flowers, fruits and garlands and roam through villages to drum up the festive atmosphere. The same night, Kama Dahan, on the lines of Holika Dahan, is held. For that, dry dung cakes, wood, coconut and betelnut, etc. are 'stolen' from the backyards of houses, as is the tradition. Stealing on this day is not an offence. By midnight, Kama, in the form of an areca sapling or a bakula branch, is set alight, and everyone dances around the flames, singing a folk song related to the occasion.

13. Usually, the Halakki Vokkaligas speak in their own dialect of Kannada, called Halakki Kannada or Achchagannada.

14. Since they were children of the forests, hunting was the Halakkis's favourite game. Following the various uprisings, peasants and villagers were denied the possession or use of certain implements and weapons by the British; consequently, they couldn't hunt. With the passing of the Indian Forest Act (1878), forests were classified as 'reserved', 'protected' or 'village'. Hunting was banned in

most parts, except for certain designated shooting blocks, which were accessible through the acquisition of a licence that was made available to very few people, most of whom were British. In order to hunt, the requisite permits would have to be obtained from the divisional forest officer of the region, who would assign shooting blocks to the applicants, but hunting for food in deeper jungles was still rampant. Owing to regulations imposed by the Indian Wildlife Act of 1972, this is now almost non-existent. Earlier, it was necessary for one person from each family to go with the group of villagers to play the hunting game and come back victorious. Hunting was also done around particular festivals, although the practice differed from one region to another.

15. 'Thaarley
    O yyoyoi maleye nammoorgei . . .
    Thaarley
    Nammoora makki Katthi batthi hwadu
    Taarle
    Dodd maLey barli
    Thaarley
    Dodd kere tumbli
    Thaarley'.

    Each line wishes for the rains to come and ensure the land flourishes.

16. 'Culture of Haalakki Vokkaligas—A Special Reference in Uttar Kannada District', Arati D. Nayak, *International Journal of History and Cultural Studies (IJHCS)*, vol. 3, no. 1, 2017.

17. Shifting agriculture.

18. It refers to a system of land tenure in which actual tillers or cultivators also have ownership or occupancy rights. In

many places where small and marginal farmers leased land from large or absentee landowners, the situation continued to be exploitative, thereby discouraging the tillers from cultivating the land efficiently. Further reading: R.V. Patil, 'All Land to the Tiller: The Problem of Land Reform in India', *Economic Development and Cultural Change*, vol. 3, no. 4, July 1955, pp. 374–80.

19. Grandmother or grandmother-like.

20. This is a rhythmic performance that has songs sung to drumbeats, mostly by men. Many of them reflect upon the lives and realities around us. They are used for upholding morality, to ensure the relationships between people of the clan remain healthy, ensuring a message of uprightness, morality and social responsibility. They can also be about legal hassles or injustice or social crimes. The songwriter wants to keep the society on the right track.

21. Dharwad is the district headquarters of Dharwad district in the state of Karnataka, India.

22. From 1965 onwards, All India Radio (AIR) is officially known as Akashavani or 'voice from the sky'.

23. Amaravati, also known as Indraloka, is the heaven of Lord Indra in Hindu mythology, with celestial gardens, sacred trees, low, sweet music and sweet-scented flowers. Often, the fragrant groves are occupied by beautiful angels known as apsaras.

## Chapter 2: The Kanjars of Chambal

1. A polite title or form of address for a man.

2. Further reading: Anastasia Piliavsky, 'A Secret in the Oxford Sense: Thieves and the Rhetoric of Mystification in Western

India', *Comparative Studies in Society and History*, vol. 53, no. 2, April 2011, pp. 290–313.

3.  M.R. Kale, trans., *Dashkumarcharitam by Dandi* (Mumbai: Sharadakridan Press, 1822).

4.  Ramacandra Varma Shastri, *Manusmṛti: Bhāratīya ācāra-saṃhitā kā viśvakośa* (Śāśvata Sāhitya Prakāśana, 1997).

5.  Burglars, highway looters, cut-purses etc. are considered to be 'secret thieves' or aprakasataskara.

6.  Kishori Saran Lal, *The History of the Khaljis A.D. 1290-1320* (New Delhi: Munshiram Manoharlal Publishers 1980).

7.  From these Bhati Rajputs emerged more nomads like Nats, Bhatus, Kanjars, Bhatu Kanjar, Bedia, Sansi, etc. In the later centuries, the Muslim rulers of Delhi—Sikander Lodi, and later Sher Shah—had to confront the lawlessness in the Chambal region, quartering the Kanjars in armed combat, that is, if they could find any.

8.  Between those years of the Maratha confederacy's bid to win an empire in India and the reality of the East India Company actually winning it was a period of turmoil. In this microcosm of time, armies were disbanded while local and regional rulers asserted themselves and Company Raj forced the issue. While the rest of society was easier to control, those who protested—especially the wandering bands of soldiers, itinerant traders and nomads, and people who registered their protest—were branded as criminals along with the other thugs. In devastating tales, these tribes, in the name of a semi-fictional cult, and in the lust for an empire, were accused and put to gallows in no less than thousands at a time.

9.  He swears on Din Devata, a deity to whom a temple is dedicated, located in Rawali, near Udaipur.

10. Baraadari also Bara Dari (Urdu: باره دری) is a building or pavilion with twelve doors on the sides of the square-shaped structure. Because of their outstanding acoustic features, these buildings were particularly well-suited for courtesan dance performances in India.

11. An obnoxious or despicable male.

12. James L. Fitzgerald, trans. and ed., *The Mahabharata*, Book 7 (Chicago: University of Chicago Press).

13. Kaccha khatiya was made by the Rajput soldiers and consumed before going into battle. Even now, the surrendered dacoits make this unlicensed liquor in the nights and sell it for about Rs 20 for a bottle in the nearby villages. It's also known as the Kanjar whiskey.

14. K.M. Kapadia, 'The Criminal Tribes of India', *Sociological Bulletin*, vol. 1, no. 2, 1952.

15. While the tribe's codes are oral, they were laid down in print by the Akhil Bharatiya Sahansmal Kanjarbhat Samaj Sangh at the Jat panchayat's Shirdi chapter in 2000. The booklet has been a de facto tribal constitution in circulation ever since. Outlawed since July 2017, the Kanjar panchayats no longer openly assemble.

16. There used to exist a secret temple in Rawali, Kota district, where hundreds of Kanjars gathered every year among friendly leopards in the thick jungles, hidden from the eyes of Kajjhas (non-Kanjars) and the law enforcers for hundreds of years. It was dedicated to the Din Devatas or the *safed ghode ke sardar*, Laluji and Dhan ji Kunwar, as the temple legend goes. They were famous dacoits who lived and prospered about four centuries ago. Before every loot, they called a bhopa, who would predict the outcome of their exploit. One fine day, despite a positive prediction, one of the men died. It was later found out

that his wife was touched by a Kajjha with a stone, and hence defiled her as well as her husband. The story could be bunk. What is strange, though, is that this story of the knights is common to criminal groups around the world. Further Reading in Italian: 'Relazione annuale sulla 'Ndrangheta', Italian Antimafia Commission, February 2008.

17. *Datura stramonium* contain tropane alkaloids in their seeds and flowers, which have been used for centuries in some cultures as a poison.

18. Ashadha or Aashaadha or Aadi is a month of the Hindu calendar that corresponds to June/July in the Gregorian calendar.

19. Frederick de L. Booth Tucker, 'The Criminal Tribes Of India', *Journal of the Royal Society of Arts, Manufactures and Commerce*, vol. 71.

20. The adopted thieves are normally expected to contribute 25–30 per cent of their loot to the patron station while the unprotected ones may need to pay double the loot amount (information obtained from compendium of the police, a document compiled and updated by the district police, which combines information collected from Kanjar informers and villagers).

**Chapter 3: The Kurumbas of the Nilgiris**

1. The Badagas are agricultural people and by far the most numerous and wealthy in the Nilgiris. Nestled within nature, they continue to practise their elaborate cultural frameworks, configuring in the modern world. They migrated from the plains of Mysuru district when a Muslim invasion destroyed the Hindu empire of Vijaynagar in AD

1565. Collectively called the Badagas, these people have a specific language called Badugu. There have been disputes related to the position of Badagas within India, since they petitioned for the Scheduled Tribe status around seventy years after being classified as a primitive tribe under the census of the 1930s.

2. M.D. Sampath, *Chittoor through the Ages* (Delhi: B.R. Publishing Corporation, 1980).

3. Gustav Salomon Oppert, *On the Original Inhabitants of Bharatavarsa or India* (Westminster: Andesite Press, 1893).

4. The paints are colours of red ('*semm manna*') and white ('*bodhi manna*'); both are soils; black is obtained from the bark of a tree ('*kari maran*') and green from the leaves of a plant ('*kaatavarai sedi*'). A piece of cloth is used to apply the colours on to the cow dung–plastered walls.

5. *Strobilanthes kunthiana*, kurinji, or neelakurinji, is a shrub that is found in the Shola forests of the Western Ghats in south India. Nilgiri Hills, which literally means the blue mountains, got their name from the purplish blue flowers of neelakurinji that blossoms only once in twelve years.

6. Semey implies regions. The four major seemeys in the Nilgiris are: Kundey, Porangadu, Toganadu and Methanadu.

7. While the Kurumbas lived deeper in the forest, the Todas and Kotas lived on the edges, and the Badagas made up the villages and towns. Except Badagas, the other three tribes were indigenous to the Nilgiris. Apart from separate occupations that made them interdependent, they each had customs, rituals, housing and clothing that differentiated them and they insist on maintaining it, in spite of their integration into each others' societies in

bigger cities and towns. Largely though, their villages still remain separate.

8. The Kurumba tribe is divided into several groups. The various groups according to many ethnographic accounts are the Jen, Mullu, Urali, Beta and Alu or Palu. The most populous of these are the Alu Kurumbas who live mainly on the Mettupalayam–Coonoor–Kotagiri–Kundah mountain stretches of Nilgiris district and in the adjoining Silent Valley/Attappady areas of Kerala. In this particular story, we refer to the Alu Kurumbas of the Nilgiris, especially the ones around Coonoor and Gudalur. Mostly, we refer to Alu Kurumbas when we use the term Kurumbas in this chapter. Further Reading: C.R. Sathyanarayanan and Nirmal Chandra, 'The Lost Landscapes and Livelihood: A Case Study of the Alu Kurumba of Nilgiris, Tamil Nadu', *Journal of the Anthropological Survey of India*, vol. 62, no. 2, 2013.

9. Further Reading: Edgar Thurston and K. Rangachari, *Castes and Tribes of Southern India* (Madras: Government Press, 1909).

10. A unique tribal trait that tends to be interpreted as a symbol of group status. Any attempt to imitate it by another group is violently resisted. For example, Badagas wear turbans; Kotas do not. When a few Kotas once took to wearing turbans, the Badagas felt that the Kotas were getting above themselves. Some of the Badagas ambushed and beat up the Kota offenders, tore off their headgear, and effectively blocked the borrowing of this trait. Further Reading: David G. Mandelbaum, *Culture Change among the Nilgiri Tribes* (Berkley: UC Berkeley Postprints from Department of Anthropology, 1941).

11. John Hutton, an English anthropologist, has suggested that a caste system 'of some sort' preceded Hinduism in India.

Although conclusive proof of this hypothesis would be
difficult to supply, acceptance of it would go a long way
towards clarifying the position of the Kurumba. The
second possibility, on the other hand, may raise more
problems than it solves. It is not easy to see how they
could have borrowed anything as fundamental and as
complex as caste through casual contact with Hindus;
and sustained contacts are so far quite unsubstantiated
in fact. Accepting the first hypothesis, however, does not
mean that the form of the caste system found among
these Dravidians today need resemble in detail some
system their ancestors held 3000 years ago. Changes of
various sorts have almost certainly occurred. However,
such questions may eventually be answered only through
an initial recognition of the Toda, Kota, Badaga and
Kurumba as 'castes' rather than 'tribes'. Further Reading:
Kota Texts: Marian W. Smith, 'A Review of the Primitive
in Indic Folklore', *The Journal of American Folklore*, vol.
61, no. 241, 1948).

12. The Alu Kurumba dances are of two types: *antes attam*
and *yenna attam*. Antes attam is performed only by male
members, whereas yenna attam is performed by females
of the community. The songs are always sung at the
time of honey collection. R. Mekala, 'Belief System and
Oral Tradition of the Kurumba Tribal', Academia.edu,
https://bit.ly/3a9b6MD

13. Sula Devaru is essentially the Hindu god Shiva. The Alu
Kurumbas are animists but it has altogether not been
possible for the Alu Kurumbas to preserve their ancestral
religious beliefs and practices without the accretion of some
Hindu ideas. They essentially had an ancestress, called
Karupade Tayi, whose benevolence and protection they

invoked by regular offerings. They live in constant fear of
evil spirits, which try to take possession of them; the fiercest
of the spirit is known as Muniravala.

14. The Nilgris are known for a peculiar kind of forest habitat
unique to the southern Western Ghats—the Sholas. The
name is derived from the Tamil for grove or forest. Moist
broad-leaved forests of stunted evergreen trees, the Sholas
occupy the higher altitudes of the southern Western
Ghats. Dense, verdant forest, usually clumped around and
overgrowing a stream, are separated by gentle undulating
meadows of short, mellow-green grasses known to be
resistant to fire and frost. The trees, such as fig, mahogany
and jamun, grow along with mosses and grasslands.

Invasive species introduced for commercial plantation
such as eucalyptus, wattle and silver oak threaten the
ecosystem, on a whole.

15. Irulas are a Dravidian ethnic group inhabiting the area of
the Nilgiri mountains, in the states of Tamil Nadu and
Kerala. A Scheduled Tribe, they are also known for their
snake-catching and honey-hunting skills.

16. The period it takes for the honey to mature is known as ittu,
or roughly speaking, from Shirkarai to Yani, in Tamil months.

17. In 1835 no less than forty-eight Kurumbas were murdered,
and a smaller number in 1875 and 1882. In 1900 a whole
family of Kurumbas was murdered, of which the head,
who had a reputation as a medicine-man, was believed
to have brought disease and death into a Badaga village.
Further Reading: Henry Harkness, *Description of a Singular
Aboriginal Race of the Neilgherry Hills* (np: Hardpress, 1832).

18. They distinguish different kinds of honey depending on the
size of the honeybee and honey's place of formation: e.g.,
*thoduva jenu* ('thoduva' means tree-top and 'jenu' means

'honey'), *betta jenu* or *hejjenu* ('betta' means 'hill-top'; 'hejja'—means 'big trees'), *kola jenu* ('kola' means 'stick'), *kallu lola jenu* ('kallu kola' denotes small boulders), Varai Jenu ('rock-holes').

## Chapter 4: The Marias of Bastar

1. Fresh ginger, garlic and red chillies mixed with crushed ants and their eggs into a paste.
2. The vigorous climbing creeper is of the family Caesalpiniaceae. The roasted seeds of this woody climber are edible.
3. Most toilets built by the government in villages around Gudari have been put to creative use, as firewood storage areas, chicken coops and even storerooms for hunting and fishing tools.
4. W.V. Grigson Humphrey Milford, *The Maria Gonds of Bastar* (np: Oxford University Press, 1938), part 1, chapter 1.
5. Ibid., Part 2, chapter 4.
6. Halbi (also Bastari, Halba, Halvas, Halabi, Halvi, Mahari, Mehari) is an Eastern Indo-Aryan language, transitional between Oriya and Marathi, spoken across the central India.
7. Gondi is spoken by two million people, including different tribal groups, across Madhya Pradesh, Gujarat, Maharashtra, Chhattisgarh, Telangana and Andhra Pradesh. It has about six dialects.
8. Magician.
9. The Anganwadi scheme was started as a rural child-care programme in 1975 as part of the Integrated Child Development Services (ICDS) programme to combat hunger and malnutrition in children and pregnant women.

10. The north region of Antagarh inhabits a larger strain of the previous inhabitants of the region, very likely the same subgroup of Maria now living in the Abujhmar hills.

11. The practice of gifting combs as an expression of desire was an age-old custom in the ghotuls, especially among the members of the Maria tribe. Some Maria villages seem to have adopted this trend too. Boys (cheliks) would spend hours carving exquisite designs on wooden combs to gift it to the girl they liked, their motiari. This tradition seems hardly in practice these days. The craft too has virtually gone extinct as plastic combs and clips in vibrant hues have replaced wooden ones.

12. The girls were barred from the ghotul during their periods which had plenty of taboos associated with it like the rest of India. They were isolated in a separate room in their homes.

13. The boys at the ghotul.

14. The ghotul seems to exist among the Maria, Jhoria and Muria tribes of Bastar region.

15. There seems to be various versions of this tale, but this seems to be the most accepted one by the Marias of Abhujmarh.

16. Further Reading: Behram H. Mehta, *Gonds of the Central Indian Highlands, Vol.1* (np: Concept Publishing Company, 1984).

17. Among the Abujmarh Marias, only boys sleep in the ghotul. The girls return home around midnight. But among the other Murias and Marias, even the girls may sleep in ghotuls and share mats with their lovers.

18. Long barrel of wood with two membranes of unequal size.

19. A large single-membrane iron drum.

20. A gong developed out of a wooden cow bell with intricate decorations.

21. As named by Verrier Elwin in the book.
22. Time for the ghotul to close.
23. The ghotul always fears a very long relationship, the comfort of which may cause a pre-marital pregnancy, which are not only socially disastrous but also alter their term at the ghotul, and complicate future marriages. The girls may have to get married to the chelik who impregnated her, and leave the ghotul, or quickly get married to the match decided by the parents if the match agrees. In that case, the chelik may continue in the ghotul after some fines and sanctions.
24. She would have to fetch firewood for the ghotul from the forest.
25. Source: Verrier Elwin.
26. Motherfucker.
27. A word that covers a variety of actions outside the ghotul which are violations of one kind or another. For example, exploiting forest resources for selfish individual benefits or a pregnancy.
28. Marias practise various methods of contraception such as coitus interruptus, avoiding sex in days immediately after the periods and, often, taking gunpowder infusions and herbs and other religious ceremonies and rituals.
29. In some ghotul, adolescents are put in monogamous relationships; in others they are discouraged from becoming emotionally attached to their partners, and those who sleep together for more than three nights are punished.
30. Verrier Elwin, *Tribal World of Verrier Elwin* (Delhi: Oxford University Press, 1964).
31. Farewell ceremony.
32. Barter system is still the traditional method of exchange among the hill Maria. Money exchange is the basic trait of

exchange. As a result, the outside traders still take the upper hand in exploiting the primitive section.

**Chapter 5: The Khasis of Shillong**

1.  Jainsem is wrapped around the body from the left, with a brooch holding its two ends together over the wearer's right shoulder; the other piece comes from under the left arm, and the two ends are fastened over the left shoulder. Each piece of cloth has a pocket on the inside, which comes in handy for Khasi women who comprise an overwhelming majority of businesspeople in the hill state.

2.  Khasi people form the majority of the population of Meghalaya, and is the state's largest community, with around 48 per cent of its population. Before the arrival of Christianity, the majority of the Khasi people practised an indigenous tribal religion. Though around 85 per cent of the Khasi have embraced Christianity, a substantial minority of the Khasi people still follow and practise their age-old indigenous religion, which is known as *Ka Niam Khasi*.

3.  During the British colonial period in the 1800s, many people from India and Bangladesh were brought to Burma to work in the British-led administration, doubling the Muslim community in fifty years. This decision was resented by the local Burmese people and forms one of the root causes of the animosity.

    World War II exacerbated this animosity. The Muslims supported the British while many Buddhists supported the Japanese. After Myanmar gained independence in 1948, the Muslims fought for equal rights, but were defeated, further solidifying the divide in their community.

One of the earliest cases of Rohingya refugees, representing the largest Muslims in the Myanmar, moving into Bangladesh dates back to 1978. Another migration occurred in the early 1990s. In each of these two instances, more than 2,00,000 Rohingya people fled Myanmar and Rakhine State.

The latest exodus began on 25 August 2017 after Rohingya Arsa militants launched deadly attacks on more than thirty police posts. Rohingyas arriving in an area known as Cox's Bazaar—a district in Bangladesh—say they fled after troops, backed by local Buddhist mobs, responded by burning their villages and attacking and killing civilians, raped and abused Rohingya women and girls. Nearly all who fled travelled to South East Asian countries, including Bangladesh, Malaysia, Indonesia and Thailand, by rickety boats via the waters of the Strait of Malacca and the Andaman Sea. They also arrived in India through its northeastern frontiers, looking for work and opportunity. Many were spotted in Shillong too.

4. Khasi is widely spoken in Shillong and written using the Latin and Bengali scripts. The main dialects of Khasi are Sohra and Shillong dialect. Shillong dialects form a dialect continuum across the capital region while Sohra dialect, due to strong colonial patronization, came to be regarded as standard Khasi.

5. Between 1979 and 1990, tribal mobs attacked Bengalis, mostly in capital Shillong, resenting their dominance in jobs and business. A Congress MLA, Manik Chandra Das, was among those killed. At least 35,000 left Meghalaya, selling off their property for a pittance, while some stayed back after spending harrowing days in relief camps. Racial attacks have not stopped. In November 2013, trader Bireshwar Das was set on fire during an agitation to demand implementation

of inner-line permit. Hindi speakers, specifically from Bihar and Rajasthan, started becoming extremist targets as 'representatives of colonial India' in the 1990s. After the 1992 attack on Biharis in Meghalaya, the B.N. Sharma Commission report said fifteen years of communal carnage in Meghalaya, beginning in 1979, displaced thousands and killed hundreds of non-tribal people in Shillong.

6. Khasi religion (Niam Khasi) used to be a dominant religion of the Khasi tribals. They believe in the Three Commandments, the Divine Laws of '*ka tip briew tip Blei*', '*ka tip kur tip kha*' and '*ka kamai ïa ka hok*' ['the knowledge of man, the knowledge of God', 'the knowledge of one's maternal and paternal relations and the earning of virtue'] Around 19 per cent of Khasis still follow the traditional religion while others have converted to other religions such as Christianity or Buddhism.

7. According to a Khasi legend, a giant serpent, U Thlen, lived in a cave that was close to a path where the villagers plied their trade. This led to many killings and disappearances until the villagers finally called U Suidnoh, who tricked the snake and managed to drop a red-hot piece of iron into the creature's mouth. The villagers then cut the snake up and devoured it to prevent the monster from regenerating itself. An old lady saved a piece of the Thlen for her son, who was away at war. Over time, this tiny piece of flesh grew back into the dangerous beast and it was free to wreak havoc on the poor villagers. The creature then took the old woman as a follower and demanded human blood and was arrested soon after for breaking the new British law against human sacrifices.

8. The then capital of united Assam before it was split from Meghalaya in 1972. It then became the capital of Himalaya.

9.  Natalie Jo-Anne Diengdoh, 'Representations of Khasi culture in mass media' (paper presented at the Seminar on Cultural Studies: Global and Local Perspectives), North-Eastern Hill University, 7 February 2015.

10. God bless you, my love, God bless you.

11. Seng Khasi is a socio-religious and cultural organization of the indigenous Khasi belonging to the Niam Khasi religion. Its aim was the protection and preservation of Niam Khasi, the customs and traditions of the indigenous Khasi which distinguishes the Khasi as a race distinct from any other race in the world. On 23 November 1899 sixteen young men decided to float Seng Khasi organization which took upon itself the work of protecting the Khasi religion, the customs and tradition and, on the whole, all aspects of pure Khasi way of life, including music, song, dance, games and amusements to ensure that its unique identity in the world is preserved for all time to come. Over the years, the Seng Khasi came to be looked upon as the source of inspiration and protection to many traditional, cultural and indigenous religions.

12. Intentionally avoiding the use of 'matriarch', because, unlike popular opinion, barely any control lies with the Khasi women on paper.

13. Sohpetbneng, the navel of heaven, according to the Khasi legend, is the umbilical cord for mortals to communicate between earth and God's abode in the sky. Sohpetbneng is twenty kilometres north of Meghalaya capital, Shillong. Every year, on the second Sunday of February, hundreds of Khasi believers trudge seven kilometres uphill from the highway to be spiritually cleansed. Through traditional rites and rituals, devotional songs and dances, they pray around

a heap of stones to appease U Blei (Creator) for the well-being of the earth and life on it.

14. Linda Chhakchhuak, 'Why Are Khasi Women Being Held Responsible for the "Dilution" of the Tribe?', The Wire, 2 August 2018.

15. Phawar is a traditional six-line Khasi verse form. It can be described as a limerick, is often humorous and expresses a thought with a point, usually satirical.

16. Animism is the religious belief that objects, places and creatures all possess a distinct spiritual essence. Potentially, animism perceives all things—animals, plants, rocks, rivers, weather systems, human handiwork and perhaps even words—as animated and alive.

17. Promanath Dutta, Impact of the West on Khasis and Jaintias (New Delhi: Cosmo Publications, 1987).

18. Tangmuri is a double-reed conical-bore wind-instrument. Duitara is a four-stringed instrument that resembles a guitar.

19. According to records, Shad Suk Mynsiem was first celebrated on 14 and 15 April 1911 at Weiking Ground to increase the scale and attract larger grounds in Mawkhar, Shillong. Ever since, the dance has been an annual ritual.

20. Shad Suk Mynsiem is the counterpart of the Garo harvest festival. Also known as the 'Dance of Contentment', the famous Shad Suk Mynsiem of Meghalaya is celebrated in the month of April at the Weiking Ground near Shillong and at other places in Meghalaya. Shad Suk Mynsiem is one of the most important tribal festivals of the Khasis. It is an annual thanksgiving dance festival, when people of the Khasis tribes offer prayer to God for the bumper harvest. Men and women, dressed in traditional fineries, dance along with the beats of drums and pipes called tangmuri,

the queen of musical instruments. The festival lasts for three days.

21. The setting represented the root of the Nniam Khasi faith, the matrilineal system, where the man provides the form and structure to a baby and the mother, its flesh and blood. For Khasis, the descent line is reckoned only by the mother's clan and a family would essentially be a great-grandmother's great-grandchildren.

22. Used in Shillong in pre-Independence days.

23. Divorce in Meghalaya is the second-highest in the country with causes ranging from incompatibility to lack of offspring, and is easily obtainable. This ceremony traditionally consists of the husband handing the wife five cowries or paisa which the wife then hands back to her husband along with five of her own. The husband then throws these away or gives them to a village elder who throws them away. Present-day Khasis divorce through the Indian legal system.

24. Jeffreyson Wahlang, 'Changes in Family and Households: Social Status and Role of Women among the Khasi Tribe of Meghalaya', Academia.edu.

25. Traditionally, post-marital residence for a married man when a heiress (known as *Ka Khadduh*) is involved must be matrilocal (that is, in his mother-in-law's house), while post-marital residence when a non-heiress is involved is neolocal. Generally, Khasi men prefer to marry a non-heiress because it will allow them to form independent family units somewhat immune to pressures from the wife's kin.

26. Traditional Khasi robes.

27. In 1942, Japan attacked Burma and ousted the British; Shillong often housed allied soldiers on the Burma front, acting as a convalescence base. Shillong was chosen for its mild weather,

general prettiness and its relative accessibility from Guwahati. The soldiers ended up staying many years after the war.

28. Covering some 192 acres, the Mawphlang Sacred Forest, nestled in the East Khasi Hills near Mawphlang village, has its roots steeped deep in the age-old religious beliefs, in which forests are regarded as a sacred entity. The local Khasi tribes have been preserving this forest for thousands of years, and believe it to be the abode of the local deity, called Labasa.

29. Local panchayat.

## Chapter 6: The Konyaks of Nagaland

1. The Angh of the village rules over more than forty-five villages that extend up to Myanmar and Arunachal Pradesh; villagers still pay nominal taxes to him.

2. The Nagas of Nagaland, and their land and resources, are protected under Article 371A of the Indian Constitution. Most of the control of the region lies neither with the government of India or Myanmar; in spite of a legislative set-up, special powers and autonomy are given to the Konyak tribe in this region to conduct their own affairs through the village council—a panchayat of sorts. Article 371A in The Constitution of India 1949 states:

Special provision with respect to the State of Nagaland

(1) Notwithstanding anything in this Constitution,

(a) no Act of Parliament in respect of

(i) religious or social practices of the Nagas,

(ii) Naga customary law and procedure,

(iii) administration of civil and criminal justice involving decisions according to Naga customary law,

(iv) ownership and transfer of land and its resources, shall apply to the State of Nagaland unless the Legislative Assembly of Nagaland by a resolution so decides.

3. The Konyaks considered head-hunting as the highest valour, and the man who could collect many heads was considered as a *naomei* or warrior. With this achievement, he could acquire the rank and tattoo of a head-taker.

4. In November 2016, the Government of India announced the demonetization of all Rs 500 and Rs 1000 banknotes of the Mahatma Gandhi Series. It also announced the issuance of new Rs 500 and Rs 2000 banknotes in exchange for the demonetized banknotes.

5. Nagamese Creole is based on Assamese, Hindi, English and Naga languages.

6. The classicist Jean-Paul Thuillier defines the Latin word *virilitas as* 'male organs'. (In Latin, *vir* can also mean just 'man' or 'husband'.) And yet *virilitas* wasn't just about size. To possess Roman virility was to radiate not just sexual power but 'virtue, accomplishment'. The virile man wasn't just sexually 'assertive', 'powerfully built' and 'procreative' but also intellectually and emotionally 'level-headed, vigorous yet deliberate, courageous yet restrained'. Giving in too often to the charms of women though was a dent in the man's virility. The concept's misogyny, of course, is more pronounced. Virility, maybe less misogynistic here than most places in India, is still interwoven with the idea of male superiority. If the men arrive at an indisputable decision, the women mostly reply with an 'Amen'.

7. The Dayak are the native people of Borneo. It is a loose term for over 200 riverine and hill-dwelling ethnic subgroups,

located principally in the central and southern interior of Borneo. The Dayak were animist in belief; however, many converted to Islam and since the nineteenth century, the Dayak were feared for their ancient tradition of head-hunting. Among the Iban Dayaks, the origin of head-hunting was believed to be meeting one of the mourning rules given by a spirit.

8.  Konyak Nagas, Christoph von Furer-Haimendorf (1969).

9.  The tribes now collectively recognized as Nagas coalesced only over the past two centuries, mainly through their encounters with outsiders. (Scholars believe the word 'Nagas' came either from the Burmese word '*naka*', meaning 'those with pierced ears', or the Assamese word '*nahnga*', meaning 'fierce warriors'.)

10. Though head-hunting raids were banned, the villagers continued to enact the hunting raids on wooden effigies and performing rites. Subsequently tattoos were marked on all the members of the age grade. This continued till 1974 when the last batch of men was tattooed in Longwa.

11. The Queen performed the work in her own house, lightly hammering and pricking the skin with the tool made from thorn bushes, while the skin was stretched by an assistant. The dents were then coated with a bluish juice made from the charred and pounded sap to enhance the blue-black pigmentation and heal the punctures.

12. Phejin Konyak, *The Konyaks: Last of the Tattooed Headhunter* (New Delhi: Roli Books, 2017).

13. Since the end of headhunting days, the villages have maintained their alliance and peace agreement with the last ambush reported in the early '90s over land disagreements. The council takes up most matters like marriage, rape

murders and village borders. Even angh's marriage and his
proposal to the girl's family and village are made by the
council. People are happy with the council as governing
body and the angh as the monarchial head.

# GLOSSARY

- Sal:              *Shorea robusta*
- Akash bel:        *Cassytha filiformis L.*
- Neem:             *Azadirachta indica*
- Chironji:         *Buchanania lanzan*
- Saja tree:        sal tree
- Angapen:          clan god
- Fita:             string
- Bilpat:           *Melochia corchorifolia*
- Nariyal:          coconut
- Supari:           areca nut
- Abbalige:         *Crossandra infundibuliformis*, the firecracker flower, is a species of flowering plant in the family Acanthaceae, native to southern India and Sri Lanka
- Sarpanch:         head of the village
- Havaldar:         police constable
- Bihads:           ravines

- ◆ Ber: *Ziziphus mauritiana* or Indian jujube
- ◆ Vaid: An Ayurvedic practitioner was called vaidya
- ◆ Rupa: armlets
- ◆ Pansgiant: crown
- ◆ *Toona ciliata*: red cedar
- ◆ Dharbha: grass
- ◆ Mahua: *Mahua longifolia*
- ◆ Salphi: sago-palm juice. Scientific name: *Caryota urens*
- ◆ Bidai: doomar or gular (*Ficus glomerata*)

# BIBLIOGRAPHY

**Chapter 1: The Halakkis of Ankola**

1. Arati D. Nayak, 'Culture of Haalakki Vokkaligas—A Special Reference in Uttar Kannada District', *International Journal of History and Cultural Studies (IJHCS)*, vol. 3, no. 1, 2017.
2. 'BuDa Folklore: Tribes of Uttara Kannada-The Halakki Tribe', 18 August 2010, https://bit.ly/2QVNG4n
3. R.V. Patil, '"All Land to the Tiller": The Problem of Land Reform in India', *Economic Development and Cultural Change*, vol. 3, no. 4, July 1955, pp. 374–380.
4. Trude Scarlett Epstein, *Economic Development and Social Change in South India* (np: publisher unknown).

**Chapter 2: The Kanjars of Chambal**

1. Anastasia Piliavsky, 'A Secret in the Oxford Sense: Thieves and the Rhetoric of Mystification in Western India', *Comparative Studies in Society and History*, vol. 53, no. 2 (April 2011), pp. 290–313.

2.  Ajay Dandekar, 'Invisible People, Inaudible Voices', *India International Centre Quarterly*, vol. 41, no.2, pp. 90–96.

3.  'Denotified and Nomadic Tribes: A Nowhere Existence', *Economic and Political Weekly*, vol. 42, no. 40 (6 October–12 October 2007).

4.  Kathryn Hansen, 'Sultānā the Dacoit and Harishchandra: Two Popular Dramas of the Nauṭankī Tradition of North India', *Modern Asian Studies*, vol. 17, no. 2, 1983, pp. 313–31.

5.  K.M. Kapadia, 'The Criminal Tribes of India', *Sociological Bulletin*, vol. 1, no. 2, 1952, pp. 99–125.

6.  Sanjay Kolekar, 'Violence against Nomadic Tribes', *Economic and Political Weekly*, vol. 43, no. 26/27 (28 June–11 July 2008).

7.  Sharon Bohn Gmelch, 'Groups That Don't Want In: Gypsies and Other Artisan, Trader, and Entertainer Minorities', *Annual Review of Anthropology*, vol. 15, 1986, pp. 307–30.

8.  S.M. Edwardes, *Crime in India* (Oxford University Press, 1924), pp. 100–01,106.

9.  W.H. Sleeman, *Ramaseeana, or a Vocabulary of the Particular Language Used by the Thugs* (Calcutta: G.H. Gutman, Military Orphan Press, 1836).

10. ———, *History of the Thugs or Phansigars of India* (Philadelphia: Carey and Hart, 1839).

11. ———, *Rambles and Recollections of an Indian Official*, 2 vols (London: J. Hatchard & Son, 1844).

**Chapter 3: The Kurumbas of the Nilgiris**

1.  A.N. Singh, Socio-Economic Survey of Scheduled Tribes in Tamil Nadu, Ooty (Tribal Research Centre, Government of Tamil Nadu, 1984).

2.  Edgar Thurston and K. Rangachari, *Castes and Tribes of Southern India* (Madras: Government Press, 1909).

3.  Gustav Salomon Oppert, *On the Original Inhabitants of Bharatvasa or India* (Westminster: A. Constable & Co.; Leipzig: O. Harrassowitz; 1893).

4.  Johann Friedrich Metz, *Tribes Inhabiting the Nilgiri Hills: Their Social Customs and Religious Rites* (Mangalore: Basel Mission Press, 1864).

5.  Paul Hockings, *A Bibliography for Nilgiri Hills of Southern India* (np: New Haven, 1978).

6.  'The Kurumbas of the Nilgiris: An Ethnographic Myth', *Modern Asian Studies*, vol. 21, no. 1, 1987, pp. 173–89.

7.  William A. Noble, 'Nilgiri Dolmens (South India)', *Anthropos*, Bd. 71, H 1./2, 1976.

**Chapter 4: The Marias of Bastar**

1.  Alice Schlegel and Herbert Barry, *Adolescence: An Anthropological Enquiry* (np: Free Press, 1991).

2.  Behram H. Mehta, *Gonds of the Central Indian Highlands, Vol. 1* (np: Concept Publishing Company, 1984).

3.  Ramachandra Guha, 'Adivasis, Naxalites and Indian Democracy', *Economic and Political Weekly*, vol. 42, no. 32, August 2007.

4.  ———, *Savaging the Civilized: Verrier Elwin, His Tribals and India* (New Delhi: Penguin Books, 2014).

5.  Sir Wilfrid Grigson, *The Maria Gonds of Bastar* (New Delhi: Oxford University Press, 1949).

6.  Verrier Elwin, *The Tribal World of Verrier Elwin: An Autobiography* (New Delhi: Oxford University Press, 1964).

7.  ———, *The Muria and Their Ghotul* (New Delhi: Oxford University Press, 1992).

8.  Walter Kaufmann, 'The Songs of the Hill Maria, Jhoria Muria and Bastar Muria Gond Tribes', *Ethnomusicology*, vol. 4, no. 3, September 1960, pp. 115–128.

9.  Website: Kamat's Pot Pourri and K.L. Kamat, 'The Ghotul System of Education', 20 January 2002, https://bit. ly/2UGLilw

## Chapter 5: The Khasis of Shillong

1.  A.K. Nongkynrih, *Khasi Society of Meghalaya: A Sociological Understanding* (revised edition) (Shillong: Galaxy Book Store, 2018), ISBN -978-81931440-9-1.

2.  Dr Barnes L. Mawrie, *The Khasis and Their Natural Environment* (Shillong: Vendrame Institute Publications, 2009).

3.  'Drug Abuse Monitoring System— A Profile of Treatment Seekers', published by MSJE, GoI and UNODC (ROSA), R -11.

4.  M.P.R. Lyngdoh, *The Festival in the History and Culture of the Khasis* (Delhi: Haranand Publication, Vikas Publishing House Pvt. Ltd, 1991).

5.  Nalini Natarajan, *The Missionaries among the Khasis* (New Delhi: Sterling Publishers Pvt. Ltd., 1977).

6.  Promanath Dutta, *Impact of the West on Khasis and Jaintias* (New Delhi: Cosmo Publications, 1987); Tiplut Nongbri, *Gender, Matriliny and Entrepreneurship: The Khasis of North-East India* (New Delhi: Zubaan Books, 2008).

7.  Sweety-Mon Rynjah, *Khasi Traditional Dancing Ornaments* (np: Ri khasi Book Agency, 2011).

8.  Tim Dyson and Mick Moore, 'On Kinship Structure, Female Autonomy, and Demographic Behavior in India',

*Population and Development Review*, vol. 9, no. 1 (March 1983), pp. 35–60.

## Chapter 6: The Konyaks of Nagaland

1. Christoph von Fürer-Haimendorf, *Konyak Nagas: An India Frontier Tribe* (New York: Holt McDougal, 1969).
2. Christoph von Fürer-Haimendorf, *The Naked Nagas* (London: Methuen & Co., Ltd., 1939).
3. Lars Krutak, *Ancient Ink* (Washington: University of Washinton Press, 2017).
4. R.R. Shimray, *Origin and Culture of Nagas* (New Delhi: Somsok Publications, 1985).

# ACKNOWLEDGEMENTS

In the many years of researching and writing this book, my daughter, all of three years by the time I finished this book, provided me with her remarkably independent behaviour and a whole lot of stickers for my laptop. My husband filled in the gaps—with his time and unconditional love and support. I also thank my mothers, both of them, for always being a call away, for mothering me long beyond their call of duty.

*White as Milk and Rice* is set in places I had never been before. If it hadn't been for the generosity, warmth, security and shelter that my hosts provided to me and my family for weeks together, I wouldn't have been able to write this book. In most cases, they also became my translators, and layered the story with perspectives and history. I'm thankful to Raman Bhatu, Nirmala Goankar, Suresh Nanjan, Amung Konyak, Namrata Naomi Rynjah and Shiv Netam. They always had enough room, food, tea and, in specific cases, incredible rice beer.

A lot of research has gone into the writing of this book and, often, I have borrowed from the experience and guidance of many.

I was immensely stirred by various foresters, constables, army men and women, taxi drivers and farmers. The young children who walk miles to reach their schools, the paths they digress, the mothers who play more roles than any jet-setting urban woman I know, and the amount of knowledge every ordinary tribal possesses about the environment they live in—trees, herbs, animals, clouds, myths, spirits and humanity.

I'm thankful to translators and scholars in their own right: Preeti Nagaraj, Pia Swer, Sweety Mon Rynjah, Ban Lyngdoh, Sobha, K. Subramanian, Jeffrey, Jyotsana Kamat, Phejin Konyak, Mani, Kari Usendi, Sukaru Usendi, N.R. Naik and Ramesh Sharma.

Maroona Murmu in the Department of History at JNU and pre-Independence anthropologists like Verrier Elwin, W.V. Grigson, Opert Gustav, Edgar Thurston and Christoph von Furer-Haimendorf for reaching impossible places long before people knew of them and documenting several important elements of tribal lives.

After every trip, I found myself in the National Library of Kolkata, digging through the immense archives with the help of their dumb waiters and sugary cups of machine coffee at the canteen. For long exchanges, I turned to my friends Jamie, Federico, Anwesha, Priyanka, Sayan Das, Prerna Kundalia and Manu Kumar, and my brother Devang. I also couldn't have done without my other friends—Rachita, Soumil, Pallavi and Khushboo—for many moments of respite and that little nudge in the right direction.

In the world of creativity, I'm lucky to have found people who take an interest in books beyond cold letters—Benyamin, Hansda Sowvendra Shekhar, Shyam Benegal, P. Sainath and Namita Gokhale. Their constant encouragement, faith and minute observations have brought this book further than I ever imagined it.

At Penguin Random House India, my publishing house for the second time in three years, had it not been for the conviction, patience and keen eyes of my editors Gurveen Chadha and Joseph Antony, this book wouldn't have taken shape. I am also grateful to the photography department for finding such a beautiful cover.

Most of all, I am obliged to the protagonists of these stories and their families. It is unfortunate than most of them could not be named, so that they could continue living their extraordinary lives in these quiet, unglorified corners of the world.